THE DEVELOPMENT, USE, AND ABUSE OF EDUCATIONAL TESTS

THE DEVELOPMENT, USE, AND ABUSE OF EDUCATIONAL TESTS

By

EDWARD BURNS, Ph.D.
Associate Professor
Programs in Professional Education
State University of New York
at Binghamton

CHARLES C THOMAS · PUBLISHER
Springfield · Illinois · U.S.A.

Published and Distributed Throughout the World by
CHARLES C THOMAS • PUBLISHER
Bannerstone House
301-327 East Lawrence Avenue, Springfield, Illinois, U.S.A.

© *1979*, by CHARLES C THOMAS • PUBLISHER
ISBN 0-398-03713-2
Library of Congress Catalog Card Number: 78-4825

Printed in the United States of America
W-2

Library of Congress Cataloging in Publication Data

Burns, Edward, 1943-
The development, use, and abuse of educational tests.

Bibliography: p. 157
Includes index.
1. Educational tests and measurements.   I.   Title.
LB3051.B796   371.2'6   78-4825
ISBN 0-398-03713-2

*To My Children, And To All Children, Who
Have Been Baptized Into The Mystique Of
Educational Testing*

PREFACE

I OFFER NO ASSURANCES that understanding educational testing will be an easy task. Testing is not simply a litany of test names, descriptions of what this test does and what that test does, or an officious account of statistics and formulas. On a series of tests Lefty received a percentile rank of 40, a stanine of 3, an IQ of 98, a raw score of 37 on a test no one could remember the name of, a grade equivalent of 2.4, and ratings of inadequate for jumping and making angels-in-the-snow. Understanding educational testing, understanding the testing of Lefty, demands a consideration of intentions and motives, of the rationale underlying test construction, of the meaning or lack of meaning conveyed by test scores, of how and why testing is part of the overall educational concept, and of Lefty. Most of all, we must consider Lefty.

Tests are often administered with great solemnity and are interpreted as if a child's dignity and potential can be transcended by a bleak, uncompromising test score. However, for those wishing to understand educational testing, for the teacher seeking direction or the parent an answer, a barrage of labels, numbers, and specialists merge to form an atmosphere of bafflement and confusion. Reading comprehension, diagnostic profiles, figure-ground performance, verbal IQ, percentile ranks, standard deviations, standard error of measurement, validity, psychologists, therapists, special teachers! What does it all mean?

The purpose of this book is to offer a perspective as to the nature and character of educational testing. An attempt will be made to explain why tests are used and abused, how tests are often deceptive and frequently misinterpreted, and why no child is little more than a composite of numbers or test scores. I hope that what is presented will offer a speck of light through the murky realm of educational testing. If my approach is too jaded or pretentious, my goal too ambitious or a misguided failure, I apologize. In any case, I ask the reader to consider that I have been baffled, beguiled, and astounded by educational testing since I was first instructed, with omnipresent eyes to discourage would-be cheaters, "Now children, fold your test booklets to the first page like I'm doing." I don't remember the exact words, but I imagine test instructions haven't changed that much over the years.

I offer no great insights, no *answer* and certainly no definitive treatise on the philosophy or pragmatic value of educational testing. I admittedly offer nothing more than an impression, comments on tests and scores, a view of educational testing and, hopefully, a degree of honesty. There will be numbers, talk of labels, and a keen eye on those involved with the test business. But I will try to remember Lefty. I will always try to keep him in mind.

ACKNOWLEDGMENTS

I WISH TO THANK Ms. Jean Limacher Burns and Ms. Sharon Raimondi for their comments concerning initial drafts of this manuscript, and the administration and faculty of Programs in Professional Education at the State University of New York at Binghamton for their cooperation and encouragement.

CONTENTS

THE DEVELOPMENT, USE, AND
ABUSE OF EDUCATIONAL TESTS

Chapter One

CHILDREN AND TESTING

HOSTILITY

Is THERE AN ANTITEST revolt in education? The idea conjures up images of meandering hordes of disgruntled students, marching on schools and campuses, chanting antitest slogans, while at the same time feverishly shredding manuals, answer sheets, and related test materials. Although Anastasi (1967) speaks of an antitest revolt ("prevalent public hostility toward testing"), the general reaction toward testing and test uses has been relatively restrained. Even a casual analysis of educational testing would reveal that test scores and tests are misused, children unfairly stigmatized, and that a person's human potential can be thoughtlessly and mechanistically reduced to a single number or score. What is truly amazing is that many practices in educational testing are so readily tolerated, that there has not been a concerted effort to depict the true character of educational testing, and that there has not been a united, thoughtful, antitest revolt.

Proponents of educational testing are quick to acknowledge that tests are far from being infallible. However, these very advocates exhibit a strong tendency to protect and justify tests rather than seeking to understand how tests can misrepresent an individual's ability or potential. As an example, Mehrens and Lehmann (1973) stated that "most of the problems related to test misuse bear upon the overgeneralizations made by users rather than because the tests per se are invalid" (p. 664). However, to accuse test users of being primarily responsible for the abuses in educational testing is a shallow oversimplification of the problem. The responsibility for the many faults associated with educational testing can be attributed to no single faction or group. Those who construct tests are responsible; those who promote and advocate tests are responsible; and, those who use tests or placidly tolerate the misuse of test scores and tests are responsible.

To understand educational testing, we must seek to evaluate testing for what it is and not for what we would like it to be. We must look at testing with concern for the individual. When we see abuses, when we discern that a facet of testing distorts our perception of another person, we must attempt to understand what exactly the distortion is, how it was caused, and why it was tolerated.

Before beginning discussion of the various components of educational testing, we might do well to pay an on-sight visit to the testing scene. As we travel through the field of testing, considerable attention will be paid to groups, averages, norms, and those elements of testing that allow us to ignore a child and his feelings. How easy it is to lose sight of the recipient of all these numbers, formulae, tests, and decisions. So just for a brief moment, let us consider the individual, the child as test taker. One might reasonably assume that the primary purpose of educational testing is to benefit the individual. This may be the greatest assumption of all.

VIGNETTES

The parking lot is full, yellow buses line the street on the west side of the school, but the noise has stopped. Herman is sitting in the third row just to the left of Mrs. Hiza's desk. Mrs. Hiza has been a kindergarten teacher for three years. She likes children, enjoys being a kindergarten teacher, and enjoys watching children grow and develop.

She sees Herman, his lips slightly parted in anticipation; she smiles and speaks to the waiting class. "Now go to the next row. Put an X on the automobile." She waits. Herman's index finger slides along the coarse paper, stops momentarily at a drawing of a truck, and then continues to the last drawing of an early model car. He holds his crayon tightly and makes a thick X on the car. "Now go to the next row. Put an X on the envelope." She pauses. Herman pauses. His lips move as he repeats to himself, "En-vel-ope, en-vel-ope." He knows, he's sure he knows, but he can't remember. A quick glance at Mrs. Hiza. She's going to ask another question. He knows she won't wait, and he experiences a flush of mild anxiety. He recognizes all three drawings—a letter with a stamp, a sheet of paper, and a pencil—but he doesn't know which to pick. "Now go to the next line. Put an *X* on the refrigerator." A last look, a hesitation, then reluctantly moving to the next series of drawings. His finger earnestly rubs the paper, down across the thick blue line that separates the rows. Mrs. Hiza . . . look at drawings . . . think hard . . . put *X* . . . across thick blue line . . . and then, finally, no more drawings. He looks up at Mrs. Hiza. "Now children close your booklets as I'm doing now." She tells the children they will rest before doing more work. Herman turns to his. friend Freddy, who is sitting to his left. "How'd you do?" he asks. "How'd you do?" Freddy asks in return. "Did you get them all right?" asks Herman. "Naw, I missed some and got some right." "Me, too. I missed some and got some right."

Herman is taking a readiness test. During the next two days he will match (SAW: WAS SAW SWA), identify letters (Put an *X* on the *w*), count (Which picture has four hats?), identify a variety of drab pictures, and do his best to draw a picture of a man. On the last day, after he has finished drawing the "best man" he can draw, he will ride home in bus number fourteen, eat half a peanut butter and jelly sandwich, drink a small glass of milk, and have a very long nap.

Mary is in the first grade and is an above average student and an adroit test taker. Her teacher stamps good papers with happy faces, and poor papers with sad faces. Mary cannot remember ever receiving a sad face. Her work is always neat, complete, and correct, and her teacher presses the happy face rubber stamp on Mary's work with great frequency. Her teacher responds by giving happy faces, and her mother by decorating the house with dittos, word sheets, fact sheets, drawings, and Mary's other first grade business.

Mary just completed her first formal achievement test. She is nervous, afraid that her work won't be in the happy face category. But she has no reason to be concerned. Her scores on the four subtests will be at the above average and superior levels. She had considerable success at forming correct sentences, matching words to pictures, reading short sentences, and adding and subtracting one digit numbers. Mary's teacher will be pleased; Mary's mother will be pleased; and Mary will be pleased. To Mary her first achievement test was not necessarily a pleasant experience, but she did find her performance—something called stanines—subject to much praise, and that made her very happy.

Louie doesn't think, much less worry, about happy faces. Last week his teacher gave the class twenty arithmetic problems of which he had seven correct. To his surprise he did not receive a sad face. Then again, he did not receive a happy face, but after a string of sad faces he was moderately satisfied. Louie did not realize that his teacher was not able to find her sad face stamp. Even if she had, he would not have been too concerned. His primary interests are basketball, two friends who live across the street, and television. He dislikes tests, dislikes taking tests, and feels no remorse when it comes to ignoring test results.

Louie is not a good test taker. He remembers last year when a lady took him into a room with a small table on which stood, in an upright position, a relatively large, square-faced mirror. He looked at pictures and said what they were; he watched her and repeated what she said. He tried but he didn't like what he was doing, and soon the slightest sound distracted him. He knew the lady didn't like it when he didn't pay attention, and he attributes that as being the reason why he hasn't seen her this year.

For a while last year, shortly after the Christmas recess, he saw the reading teacher. Recently, however, he has not seen her. This pleases him. He tried to make her happy by doing the exercises, but he always said the words wrong, and she would get mad, and he would want to leave. And then the questions! Always reading, always questions. She would shake her head, contort her lips in desperation, until he finally yelled, "Stop!" He screamed, "Stop doing that!" That was the last time he saw the reading lady.

Louie is certainly not a good test taker. He did horrendously on his readiness test, talked incessantly during the vision and hearing screening, was among the lowest on the last achievement test, and had the unfortunate luck of not doing well on an individual test of intelligence. Louie wasn't aware that he was undergoing a psychological examination, but something he did during that experience would forever affect his formal education. "What is a camel?" asked the psychologist. Louie's mind wandered. What's he asking? What's in that box? What's he writing? "What is a camel?" the psychologist repeated. Louie shrugged his shoulders, rolled his eyes, and replied, "Some kinna animal." Louie thought the psychologist would never stop. "How many hours in a day? Grass is green, sugar is————? Put that picture together. Copy these blocks." Then the psychologist asked, "Repeat after me: nine . . . five . . . seven . . . one." Louie didn't respond. He looked right into the eyes of the psychologist, beyond his glasses, and grinned. He did not speak, he did not answer, he only grinned A barely perceptible shade of red touched the psychologist's face and quickly disappeared, and Louie's psychological examination was over.

Have you ever wondered how a child feels when he is being tested? Or what a child thinks? These are difficult questions and generally avoided by the test-minded community. Does a child know that certain tests are very serious, and that he should be very serious, and that if he is not, he might be placed in a special classroom? Does a small child become angry? Does he say, "I know more than this; I can do something else; I am more than these questions?" After the ritual of distributing tests, after the impersonal instructions, when heads are bent and responses made, how does a child come to grips with lack of interest, anxiety, and the retrieval of bits of facts and experiences strewn about his mind?

To consider the complete individual is not simply important, it is essential. A six-year-old child commented after completing a multipart examination that the test was horrible, that he didn't like it, and it gave his friend a headache. He did not refer to the test as a "test," but only as "the hard work" he was required to do for his teacher. To understand this six-year-old's test behavior, we must understand the individual. Likewise, to understand the performance, reactions, and decisions regarding Herman, Mary, and Louie, we must constantly remind ourselves that each is an individual, each is unique, and that each is far more complex than whatever information might be conveyed by a test score.

Herman survived his readiness test—to a degree, that is. His test, and the tests of the other children, were enclosed in a large envelope by the teacher, carefully sealed, sent to the company that produced the test, scored, and the results were returned to the school principal. Herman received a raw score of 35, which placed him in the below average group. The raw score indicates that of the 75 problems on the test he answered 35 correctly. Mr. Fredrickson, the school principal, knew this placed Herman in the below average category because the manual specifically stated that children with scores between 15 and 35 were in the below average category. There was no escaping the obvious; it was right there in the manual.

Herman, as he would surmise later, had a problem because he was in the below average category. Mr. Fredrickson had a problem because he was responsible for grouping children into three first grade classes: above average, average, and below average. Mr. Fredrickson's reasoning concerning grouping children into three classes according to ability level was not without merit. Years ago he logically concluded that above average children should be in the above average class, average children should be in the average class, and below average children should be in the below average class. His logic was biting and, in addition, his teachers demanded grouping. They said they couldn't teach unless the children were grouped. "After all," they said, "how can we teach reading? You don't expect us to individualize for each and every child?" So Herman was placed in the below average class, and wouldn't you know, his parents got wind of his first grade placement. They marched into Mr. Fredrickson's office and asked, "Why is Herman in the slow class?" Mr. Fredrickson smartly contended that Herman received a score of 35 on the readiness test, and that the score placed Herman in the slow class.

Mr. Fredrickson liked this reasoning. He didn't place Herman in the slow class; what his teachers wanted didn't place Herman; Herman's score on a readiness test placed him. Parents have been known to be critical of school principals or teachers, but who would dare impugn the integrity of a test score. The parents, being parents, were still skeptical. They wanted the best for their Herman, and a below average first grade placement did not occur to them as being beneficial to Herman's education. Mr. Fredrickson rectified their lack of insight as to the workings of a complex professional educational system. He emphasized the merits of Herman's slow classroom placement. "He will have upward mobility," he said straight faced. He explained that if Herman were in the top class, he wouldn't have anywhere to go, but in the slow class he could always go up. He further explained that children in the below average readiness category, of which a raw score of 35 was a part, would have difficulty succeeding in first grade and needed to be placed in a below average class in order that special help could be provided. Herman's parents finally consented to the placement. If that was what Herman needed, what else were they to do?

They left before Mr. Fredrickson had time to explain that if Herman had received a score of 36 instead of 35 he would have been placed in the average group. This meant, according to the readiness test manual, that Herman would have a good chance of succeeding in the first grade. He also forgot to mention that children assigned to the below average first grade class would, in all probability, remain in slow groups for the duration of their educational careers—although there truly was the possibility of upward mobility. Mr. Fredrickson also thought it best not to mention that children in the slow class were easily distracted (certainly not that a teacher might be uninteresting) and that a "special" effort was needed to keep the children in their seats. And of course there was the problem of grouping. Certainly Herman's parents would not be interested in the fact that he had no choice but to group and that some children, regardless of what they knew or what they might do, had to be placed in the slow class. Finally, Mr. Fredrickson did not tell Herman's parents an important fact because he himself did not know. Herman happened to be a very cautious child, and he was very cautious on his readiness test and did not guess at answers he did not know. If he had, in all likelihood, he would have been assigned to the average class.

Mary has a flare for school and test taking. To the surprise of no one, Mary did well on her first formal achievement test.

This made her happy, her parents happy, and her teacher happy. Mary was elated because, like most individuals, she likes to excel, to be proficient, and to stand out so as to shout out her individuality. Mary's parents are happy because they love Mary. They want the best for Mary, and a good education is a necessary beginning. Mary's teacher is pleased because she feels she accomplished her job; she feels a sense of competence and satisfaction through Mary's success. There was little doubt when Mary was first placed in the above average class whether or not she would succeed. One hopes that Mary's success transcends her high test scores, that she grows to develop an imaginative, sensitive, resourceful mind, and that doing well on tests is not the purpose and end of her schooling. One also hopes that Mary learns that for above average students test scores can also distort what an individual is and what an individual is capable of becoming.

Louie is what you would call a loser. You might find it difficult to imagine a bona fide loser beginning with kindergarten, but Louie is a very special case. First of all, he had the bad luck of having parents who weren't especially fond of one another, much less of Louie. They were poor, their vocabularies were poor, and Louie's father was an alcoholic. Louie now accepts his father's behavior—an eight-year-old is usually not surrounded by options regarding the quality of his existence. But when he was in kindergarten, when he was smaller, he remembers his father coming home drunk, and the filthy words and his mother's blank stare, and this bothers him. It bothered him when he took his readiness test.

Louie didn't always sleep well, he was frequently hungry, and his clothes were in a sorry state. No one was the least surprised when Louie was placed in the below average class. But for some reason Louie did not experience upward mobility. He was dismissed from speech therapy because he needed more help than the therapist could provide. She only had fifteen minutes to work with Louie a week, and that was hardly enough time to work with a child like "that." The speech therapist did not define "that." Furthermore, she offered diagnostically, she thought that the boy was mentally retarded; "just look at him," she would say. He was dismissed from remedial reading for screaming at his reading teacher an incomprehensible, savage warning to "Stop doing that!" And subsequently calling her a "bitch." Louie's father, after all, was not that bad of a teacher. Finally, after so many complaints, Louie was examined by the school psychologist and was found to have an IQ low enough to place Louie in a class for the educable mentally retarded. When Louie's former speech therapist heard of Louie's designation, she thought of herself as a very perspicacious and insightful clinician. When the psychologist was told that Louie was placed in a class for the educable mentally retarded, he felt a twinge of satisfaction that no one would ever detect. And that's what happened to Louie.

ELEMENTS OF TRUTH

The difficulty involved with understanding test scores, tests, and the role of educational testing stems from the entanglement of elements of truth, good intentions, and usefulness with outright deception, an unfathomable disregard for human potential, and damned idiocy. The character of educational testing runs the gamut from commendably beneficial to inexcusably nonsensical. There is no question that testing can contribute to individual growth and the maximization of individual potential. A hearing loss is detected, and a child's residual hearing is maximized and, if necessary, special skills are provided; why a child has difficulty reading is determined; areas where a child has difficulty achieving are delineated; problem solving, learning, and level of conceptualization are assessed so that the most suitable educational experiences can be provided.

Just as educational testing can be immeasureably beneficial, there are also minor hazards and occasions of deplorable abuse. Tests are given for the sake of testing; tests are used to provide a cacophony of pseudoscientific labels; tests are used to exclude a child from a normal educational setting; tests are used to distort a child's ability, or tests encourage an environment where potential is secondary to a test score.

Testing is naturally a very broad topic, and a listing of the various merits and limitations would be a rather formidable task, that is if all the merits and limitations of testing were known. Although many would subscribe to one of Webster's (1976) definitions of a test ("an ordeal or oath required as proof of conformity with a set of beliefs"), Cronbach (1970) stated that "a test is a systematic procedure for observing a person's behavior and describing it with the aid of a numerical scale or category-system" (p. 26). In short, some aspect of a person's behavior or existence is evaluated, and a score is given. In the best interests of testing, this is done objectively, methodically, and with no malice intended.

The sheer variety and quantity of tests available are astonishing. There are formal tests, informal tests, verbal tests, IQ tests, achievement tests, reading tests, social studies tests, writing tests, personality tests, perceptual motor tests—the categories of tests, and the number of tests within each category, are mind boggling. In subsequent chapters, particular attention will be paid to the rather large category of tests that are said to be standardized. A standardized test generally has specific materials, forms, instructions, scoring procedures, and norms. In addition, standardized tests are usually accompanied by a test manual containing varying amounts of statistical data to support the' merits of the test. Finally, and this is most important, standardized tests are usually sold; that is, the construction, promotion, and sale of standardized tests is affected not only by altrusim, but also by necessary and understandable business considerations.

One of the possibilities of which you as the reader must be aware is that in attempting to describe distortions and misinterpretations, the present account of educational testing might itself be a distortion and a misinterpretation. Ebel (1964), in describing critics of educational testing, stated that "what appears in print often seems to be only an elaboration and documentation of prejudices and preconceptions, supported by atypical anecdotes and purposefully selected quotations. Educational testing has not fared very well in these articles" (p. 425). Nothing in educational testing is black and white, and should you find fault with the present interpretation of test scores and tests, or with test uses and practices, it is your responsibility to be critical and to comment. Most important, you should not be intimidated by "experts," cowered by the saintly countenance of statistics, or be frightened by the task of seeking honesty in educational testing. When a child is concerned, all tests, including standardized tests, are really of quite secondary importance.

Chapter Two

DECEPTIVE HIERARCHIES

RANKING CHILDREN

W E IN THIS COUNTRY have a penchant for ranking. Football and baseball players are ranked, tennis players are ranked, presidents are ranked, *Time* magazine ranks pretty much everything, and children are ranked. One of the most popular methods for indicating a child's performance on a test is to assign a percentile rank and thus show the percent of children who scored above that child and the percent of children who scored below that child. As an example, a child correctly identified twenty-six words on a reading vocabulary test. The teacher reported that a score of twenty-six was equivalent to a percentile rank of 84. This can be interpreted to mean that 84 percent of the children scored lower than twenty-six, or, conversely, 16 percent of the children scored higher than twenty-six. A second child received a raw score of nineteen and a percentile rank of 43. This can be interpreted to mean that 43 percent of the children scored below a score of nineteen or that 57 percent of the children scored above nineteen.

The concept of percentile rank is relatively easy to comprehend. The only immediate concern is defining the children who scored lower or higher. In some instances the children referred to will be those who took the test with the child, while on other occasions the children referred to will be those in the school, the school district, or children from schools across the country. If someone scored lower or higher than a child, it is important to know who that someone is.

We can better explore the meaning of percentile ranks, and how children's test scores are used to determine percentile ranks, by examining the test efforts of a person intimately involved with

14

test construction. Doctor K, a professor at a large metropolitan university, devised what he considers to be a novel, short-form reading test. Doctor K did this for the following reasons: he wished to further his name in his chosen field; he desired to supplement his income; and the university had said that he had better produce (the common expression being "publish or perish") or start looking for employment elsewhere. He decided to develop a short-form test because he felt that this would be an efficient and inexpensive method for evaluating reading. Furthermore, his own past research indicated that a short-form reading test had what he cryptically called "appealing statistical properties." In addition, a short-form test would be easy to develop as well as having great appeal to those looking for a simple method for evaluating reading. Doctor K has an eye for business.

Doctor K's test consists of four words. Unfortunately, the exact four words used by Doctor K cannot be revealed since that might lead to public dissemination and test invalidation. However, the words used by Doctor K were on the order of DOG, BLUE, MOTHER, and CLOSE.

The test is easy to administer. The subject is shown a word (each is printed on glossy 5 by 8 inch cards), the word is read, and the response is recorded by the examiner. The "subject" referred to is actually a child, but Doctor K considers himself a researcher and has a decided preference for scientific-sounding terminology. The examiner, as one might well imagine, is the person who gives (or administers as is said in testing) the test.

Doctor K's test, which is called the SWRT (pronounced *swirt* and an acronym for Short Word Reading Test) was standardized on a group of twenty-five children, purchased by a publisher, and put on the market for the low, low price of $2.95. The complete test kit includes a sheet of instructions and a norm table (this comprises what might loosely be termed the test manual), four 5 by 8 inch glossy word cards, and fifty scoring forms.

Mrs. Grouper, after reading several attractive advertisements for the SWRT, purchased the kit by mail through the United States Testing Corporation so that she could quickly identify children having reading problems. Subsequently, she administered the test to three children and their scores were one, zero, and two. The norm table (Table I) revealed that a raw score of zero was equivalent to a percentile rank of 2, a raw score of one was equivalent to a percentile rank of 16, and a raw score of two was equivalent to a percentile rank of 50.

TABLE I

PERCENTILE RANK NORMS FOR THE SWRT

Raw Score	Percentile Rank
4	98
3	84
2	50
1	16
0	2

Mrs. Grouper inspected the scores and corresponding percentile ranks and was puzzled. How, she mused, could a child receive a score of zero and still have a percentile rank of 2? And how could one correct answer result in a jump from a percentile rank of 16 to a percentile rank of 50? And now that she has given the SWRT to her class, just what do the results mean?

PERCENTILE RANKS

The case of the SWRT is, of course, fictitious but not necessarily that preposterous. Parents, teachers, and professionals are frequently faced with the prospect of interpreting a stark percentile rank with little explanation as to what that percentile rank means or how it can be misinterpreted. An analysis of how Doctor K developed his table of norms will reveal an exceedingly logical procedure, logical results, and a fairly clear explanation as to why and how percentile ranks can be so misleading.

The first step is to consider Doctor K's sample of 25. Standardized tests will generally have samples ranging between 100 and 1000 for a particular age group, so a sample of 25 is very, very small. In some cases samples of less than 100 will be used, and in many cases sample sizes will go well beyond 1000. The sample and sample size must always be kept in mind, because this will be the basis for evaluating the performance of children who subsequently take the test. Many tests give the impression that raw scores correspond to indisputable, "made-up-in-heaven" percentile ranks. Not so. When a child receives a score on a test, that score is usually evaluated with respect to the performance of a standardization sample (norm group). If a standardization sample had been drawn from New York City, and the test was administered to children living in Grand Rapids, Michigan, one would have to justify, at least in his/her own mind, the legitimacy of using that standardization sample as a frame of reference. Similarly, if the size of the standardization sample was very small, one would surely question the representativeness of the sample. By chance alone, a small sample might be comprised of predominantly brighter children, children of one sex, or children from a narrowly defined socioeconomic background. Generally speaking, larger samples are preferred to smaller samples, although there are instances when even the composition of extremely large samples is suspect.

Having considered the sample, the method by which percentile ranks are determined can now be evaluated. The raw data used by Doctor K are presented in Table II.*

TABLE II

SWRT RAW SCORES AND SECRET CODES FOR
25 FICTITIOUS CHILDREN

Child	Raw Score	Child	Raw Score
AJ	2	ER	3
KM	0	KN	1
PR	3	RG	3
RT	1	TG	2
EG	3	HA	2
JL	4	DN	2
AF	2	JH	1
TD	2	PS	2
BF	1	RY	3
QB	1	NG	1
CC	2	AZ	2
AF	2	MI	3
OV	2		

* Examples have been constructed to best convey the meaning and purpose of statistical techniques and procedures, and not to exemplify research methodology current in educational testing. Research studies in educational testing may have very little meaning or import, but authors do adhere to fairly rigorous methodological principles. An important rule to remember in educational testing research is that usefulness and meaningfulness are secondary to exactness and statistical agility.

Under the column headed *child,* initials indicate each of the twenty-five children who took the SWRT. As as example, child AJ (The initials suggest a gradual transition from concern for the individual to concern for the group.) received a raw score of 2; that is, he was able to correctly identify two of the four words. Child KM, on the other hand, incorrectly identified all four words presented.

Using the SWRT data shown in Table II, the exact method for determining percentile ranks is presented in Table III. The first column in Table III indicates the five possible raw scores a child could receive on the SWRT: 4, 3, 2, 1, and 0. The first step is to determine how frequently each score occurred. This is done by noting each raw score and then putting a tally mark next to that raw score on the percentile rank work sheet. A score of 4 only occurred once (child JL) and so there is only one tally mark next to a raw score of 4 in Table III. However, eleven children received scores of 2, resulting in eleven tally marks adjacent to that raw score.

The third column, the frequency column, indicates how frequently each score occurred. This is simply the sum of tally marks. The next column is the *cumulative frequency* column, and this is found by successively adding the frequencies in the *frequency* column. The entries under the *cumulative frequency* column in Table III were found as follows: $1 = 1$; $1 + 6 = 7$; $1 + 6 + 11 = 18$; $1 + 6 + 11 + 6 = 24$; $1 + 6 + 11 + 6 + 1 = 25$.

TABLE III

HOW DOCTOR K FOUND PERCENTILE RANKS

Raw Score	Tally	Frequency	Cumulative Frequency	Cumulative Frequency Midpoint	Divide by N*	Multiply by 100
4	I	1	25	24.5	.98	98
3	╫╫ I	6	24	21.0	.84	84
2	╫╫ ╫╫ I	11	18	12.5	.50	50
1	╫╫ I	6	7	4.0	.16	16
0	I	1	1	0.5	.02	2

*N = 25

These entries indicate how many children received scores up to and including a given score. Eighteen children received scores up to and including a raw score of 2, while all 25 children received scores up to and including a raw score of 4.

Thus far the calculation of percentile ranks has been a straightforward task. Now, however, an assumption must be made before final percentile ranks can be determined. A percentile rank indicates the percent of scores above or below a given raw score. In Table III it is seen that 6 children received a raw score of 3. To find the percentile rank associated with a raw score of 3, we must assume that half of these 6 children were actually above a raw score of 3 and half were somewhat below a raw score of 3. The assumption that some children were actually above or below a raw score of 3 does not mean that we are assuming that they had scores as high as 4 or as low as 2. Rather, we assume that if the test were extremely sensitive, some children would have scores of 3.1, 3.2 and the like, whereas other children would have scores slightly below three (e.g., 2.9, 2.8). This assumption allows us to state that a percentile rank indicates the percent of scores above or below a given raw score.

The last important phase of calculating percentile ranks involves employing our assumption about children being slightly above and below scores and determining the *cumulative frequency midpoint*. The cumulative frequency midpoints shown in Table III were found by dividing a frequency corresponding to a raw score by 2 and then adding to this the total number of scores below that raw score. Thus, the cumulative frequency midpoint of 0.5 was found by dividing the frequency corresponding to a raw score of 0 by two and adding the number of cases below 0: $1 / 2 = 0.5$; $0.5 + 0$ (the number of scores below 0) $= 0.5$. The cumulative frequency of 12.5 associated with a raw score of 2 was found as follows: $11 / 2 = 5.5$; $5.5 + 7$ (the number of cases below a raw score of 2) $= 12.5$.

Finally, to find percentile ranks, each cumulative frequency midpoint was divided by the total number of children and then multiplied by 100. This final effort reveals that a raw score of 4 has a percentile rank of 98; a raw score of 3 a percentile rank of 84; a raw score of 2 a percentile rank of 50; a raw score of 1 a percentile rank of 16; and a raw score of 0 a percentile rank of 2. In the present example the median is a raw score of 2. This is the point at which 50 percent of the scores are above and 50 percent of the scores are below. As indicated, a raw score of 2 is associated with a percentile rank of 50.

The example of the SWRT is unusual for two reasons. First, the SWRT is ridiculously short. Although statistical data supporting the use of a test this short could almost certainly be found, having a child attempt to identify four words would hardly provide sufficient information to understand a child's reading behavior—such is the difference between statistical use and sensible use. Second, the distribution of SWRT scores is perfectly symmetrical. SWRT raw scores and corresponding frequencies were plotted in Figure 1. As can be seen by the line connecting the five points (thus the shape of the distribution), there is a perfect balance between frequencies above and below the median. This situation rarely, if ever, occurs. A more typical example are the raw scores, frequencies, and percentile ranks shown in Table IV and portrayed in Figure 2. The range of raw scores (from a low of 26 to a high of 45) is respectable, and the shape of the distribution lacks the evenness and symmetry of SWRT scores. There is no way to portray a typical norm table, or typical frequencies, or what a typical distribution of scores might look like. The only prudent approach to this problem is to assume that anything is possible in educational testing, that one must constantly seek to understand and never underestimate, and that bizarre and strange findings are not remote from testing.

MISINTERPRETATIONS

There is nothing intrinsically devious or misleading about percentile ranks. They provide a means to rank children, to say that a child scored higher than 20 percent, or 50 percent, or 99 percent of the children who comprised the standardization sample. The difficulties surrounding percentile ranks most often center around their use without due consideration for what information is being conveyed and the failure to consider percentile ranks that obviously distort a child's performance.

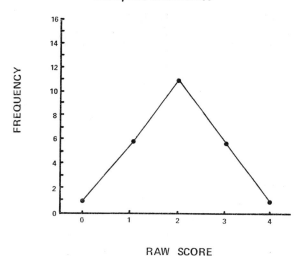

RAW SCORE

Figure 1. The symmetrical distribution of SWRT scores.

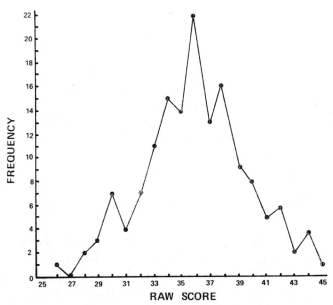

Figure 2. A typical example of a symmetrical frequency distribution.

TABLE IV

EXAMPLE OF PERCENTILE RANK TEST NORMS AND THE
UNDERLYING FREQUENCY DISTRIBUTION

Raw Score	Frequency	Percentile Rank
45	1	99
44	4	98
43	2	96
42	6	93
41	5	90
40	8	85
39	9	80
38	16	71
37	13	62
36	22	50
35	14	38
34	15	28
33	11	20
32	7	14
31	4	10
30	7	6
29	3	3
28	2	1
27	0	1
26	1	—

Concerning the matter of interpretation and the impression that a percentile rank might make, parents are frequently required to interpret percentile ranks without a shred of guidance. A report is sent, and percentile ranks are reported for a variety of academic areas (e.g., reading, arithmetic, language). Tommy receives a percentile rank of 63 on a subtest entitled "Language Usage." Tommy's mother thinks that knowing only 63 percent of the questions is not very good, and she is concerned. But a percentile rank is not a percentage, and such confusion as to the meaning of percentile ranks can only be avoided by providing parents with all necessary information to interpret percentile ranks.

Tommy's mother speaks to Tommy's teacher about his low score in language usage. Tommy's teacher politely informs Tommy's mother that a percentile rank is not a percentage, but rather a percentile rank of 63 means that 63 percent of the chidlren scored below that score. Tommy's mother leaves moderately satisfied thinking that Tommy scored higher than 63 percent of the children in his class. This is not necessarily so. Tommy's percentile rank may refer to a national sample. If this is the case, Tommy scored higher than 63 percent of the children who comprised the national sample and not higher than 63 percent of the children who took the test when he did. For all Tommy's mother knows, a percentile rank of 63 may be the highest (or lowest) percentile rank in his class. If information cannot be provided that will allow a parent or teacher to interpret a percentile rank, then percentile ranks should not be given in the first place.

One of the most common criticisms of percentile ranks is that the difference between raw score points and corresponding percentile rank points is not equal. As an example, on the SWRT (Table III) a percentile rank of 2 is equivalent to a raw score of 0, a percentile rank of 16 is equivalent to a raw score of 1, and a percentile rank of 50 is equivalent to a raw score of 2.* The difference between raw scores of 0 and 1 is 14 percentile rank points while the difference between raw scores of 1 and 2 is 34 percentile rank points. However, we cannot say that a child who received a percentile rank of 16 was more similar to a child who received a percentile rank of 2 than to a child who received a percentile rank of 50. A child who received a percentile rank of 16 scored only one point higher than a child who received a percentile rank of 2 and only one point lower than a child who received a percentile rank of 50. Percentile ranks do not always reflect raw score differences.

The general finding that raw scores have larger percentile rank differences near or around the mean results from the fact that most individuals usually score near or around the mean; that is, scores become less frequent the farther they are from the mean. If we gave a test to 100 children and 10 received a score of 3, 80 received a score of 2, and 10 received a score of 1, we would find that a score of 3 was equivalent to a percentile rank of 95, a score of 2 was equivalent to a percentile rank of

---

* Percentile refers to a score (e.g., the 15th percentile is a score of 25), while percentile rank indicates the proportion of scores below or above a given point (e.g., the percentile rank of a reading score of 56 is 70; that is, 70% have scores below a raw score of 56 and 30% have scores above a raw score of 56).

50, and a score of 1 was equivalent to a percentile rank of 5. Although a child with a score of 3 would be 45 percentile rank points higher than a child with a score of 2, the fact remains that there is still only a one-point difference between their raw scores. The raw score difference can be small, but the percentile rank difference can be quite large.

The only practical method for interpreting percentile ranks is to inspect their corresponding raw scores. On a standardized test a child received a percentile rank of 35. Is this child below average? An inspection of the percentile ranks and corresponding raw scores for this test reveals that if the child had answered correctly three additional questions, he would have had a percentile rank of over 50. A percentile rank of 35 appears to be low, but remembering that only three more questions answered correctly would have resulted in an "average" score puts this child's test performance in proper perspective.

Advice to inspect the relationship between raw scores and percentile ranks is easier to give than to follow. Percentile ranks are given, but rarely are the underlying test norms (the table showing the correspondence between raw scores and percentile ranks) made available for public information. Where does one obtain a table of norms for a test that a child has been given? The school should have at least one copy of the test manual and test norms, although this information may be tucked away in a file cabinet gathering dust. Such information does exist, and if you wish to understand a percentile rank, you must find and understand the source from which it came. Never, under any circumstances, should a percentile rank be accepted at face value.

There is no index or statistic that is not subject to certain limitations, including percentile ranks. However, there are occasions when percentile ranks are so inappropriately used that minor limitations become mammoth distortions. Consider the case of skewed score distributions. When scores on a test extend farther in one direction than in the opposite direction, the scores are said to be skewed. If the range of higher scores exceeds the range of lower scores, the distribution is said to be skewed to the right or positively skewed (positively as in "+" and not as in "definitely"). If the range of lower scores exceeds the range of higher scores, the distribution is said to be skewed to the left or negatively skewed. Another way to assess skewness is to compare the mean and median. If the mean of a test is greater than the median, the distribution is positively skewed. If the median of a test exceeds the mean, the distribution is negatively skewed.

Figure 3 presents a distribution that is negatively skewed. A distribution such as this most commonly occurs when a test is too easy. A large number of children receive the highest possible score (10), and then the scores taper off in a downward direction.

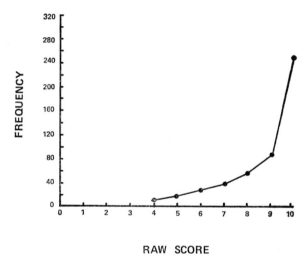

RAW SCORE

Figure 3. A negatively skewed frequency distribution.

The raw scores, frequencies, and percentile ranks for the distribution shown in Figure 3 are presented in Table V. As can be seen, a perfect score is equivalent to a percentile rank of 75, while one incorrect (a score of 9) is equivalent to a percentile rank of 41. The relatively low percentile rank for a perfect score is due to the "splitting up" of rankings of the highest scoring children. Remember that a percentile rank indicates the percent higher or lower than a given score. Two hundred and fifty children (or 50% of the sample) have scores lower than 10. If there were 250 children with scores of 10, we would assume that half have scores slightly higher than 10, and half have scores slightly lower than 10. One half of 250 (half the children with a raw score of 10) plus 250 (the number of children with scores below 10) is 375. Three hundred and seventy-five divided by 500 is .75, and multiplied by 100 is 75. The results were not in error. A perfect score is equivalent to a percentile rank of 75.

TABLE V

EXAMPLE OF PERCENTILE RANKS BASED ON A
SKEWED FREQUENCY DISTRIBUTION

Raw Score	Frequency	Percentile Rank
10	250	75
9	90	41
8	60	26
7	40	16
6	30	9
5	20	4
4	10	1

The absurdity of using markedly skewed distributions as a basis for determining percentile ranks may seem unlikely but the practice does certainly occur. One can only surmise why an individual constructing a test would provide norms that could be so misleading. One explanation might be that the earning capacity of a test increases in relation to the population for which the test is designated. There are certain earning limitations to a test suitable for only second graders. However, if the test were said to be suitable for third, fourth, and fifth graders as well—the potential for selling more tests is all too obvious. But would the test be too easy for fourth and fifth graders? Possibly. And if it is too easy, a perfect score might be equivalent to a percentile rank of 75, and one incorrect might be equivalent to a percentile rank of 41. There is often more to the origin and use of percentile ranks than meets the eye.

With all their limitations and their potential for misinterpretation, why are percentile ranks still used to interpret a child's test performance? The answer to this question is one of the more paradoxical explanations in the annals of educational testing.

Percentile ranks are used because they are easily interpreted, very descriptive, and easly understood by individuals unfamiliar with the intricacies of testing. A test manual will expertly cite the many disadvantages and limitations of percentile ranks and then condescendingly explain that they are included for those not skilled in testing.

A percentile rank alone is meaningless. To understand a percentile rank, one must understand the test, the test items, and the norms to which the percentile rank refers. There is no excuse for a lack of information when the well-being of a child is concerned. If a percentile rank is misleading, if a percentile rank is used to distort what a child is or what a child can do, it is the result of blind and unwarranted faith in the probity and usefulness of test scores. A child is more than a percentile rank, and to insure that this is not forgotten, parents, teachers and professionals involved with understanding a child's test performance have a primary obligation to determine what such a score does and does not reveal.

Chapter Three

A STORY OF STANDARD SCORES

AVERAGE CHILDREN

W HAT IS AN average child? Statements are made that "he's doing about average," or that "he's a fairly average child," but what is really meant? To some, average might mean "no special attention needed," and to others "normal," while to still others "blah." Average children, of which no child could philosophically be excluded, are readily accepted but rarely praised for their "averageness."

The concept of "average" or "normal" is important only in that some children are said to be "above average," "below average," or "not normal." Although a child might be said to be "below average" and "not normal" (abnormal) for the same reason (a score on a test), this does not mean that being "below average" is the same as being "not normal." A child might be an average swimmer, an above average listener, but a below average solver-of-arithmetic-word-problems. A child is below average "in something," but when a child is said to be "not normal," his whole being is affected. As an example, a child might be below average on a test, and he might also be below average in certain school subjects. The test, however, might be held in such awe that to be below average on this test suggests to school personnel that the child is not merely below average, but not normal as well. Being "below average" indicates performance, while being "not normal" implies general inferiority.

As important as the concept of average is, there have been few attempts to define an average child. The inability to list what is necessary to be average is understandable in view of the many possibilities. One could say that an average child eats breakfast, does not want to eat breakfast, asks questions, laughs, talks, has friends, waits for a school bus, walks to school, asks questions, is excited before Christmas, learns to read, occasionally has trouble learning to read. . . . Average by almost any standard is a very elusive concept.

A normal or average child may be difficult to define, but there have been several attempts. Otis (1925) stated that "a child of ten years is said to be exactly normal if his score is the median of the scores of 10-year children" (p. 141). This is an old reference, but the idea should be nonetheless clear. If a child's score on a test is higher than 50 percent of the other scores, then the child is said to be normal. The question remains, of course, as to what a child is called if his score is not the median—not exactly normal?

Kirk and Paraskevopoulos (1969), in describing the "average children" used as the standardization sample for the Illinois Test of Psycholinguistic Abilities (Kirk, McCarthy, and Kirk, 1968), offered the following: "only those children demonstrating average intellectual functioning, average school achievement, average characteristics of personal-social adjustment, sensory-motor integrity, and coming from predominantly English-speaking families" (pp. 51-52). This definition rests not so much on what average is, but how far above or below the average will be tolerated. In other words, if we say that only children with "average intellectual functioning" will be considered, we must state the limits of "averageness." The authors of this test designated children with IQs between 84 and 116 as being in the "average" intellectual functioning range. As to children "coming from predominantly English-speaking families," the concept of "average" is relative, and in the valley of the blind the sightless are average.

Terman and Merrill (1973, p. 17-18), in discussing a scheme for interpreting IQ scores derived from the Stanford-Binet intelligence scale, stated that IQs in the 90 to 109 range are in the average range. They also noted that approximately 46 percent of IQs will be in this "average" range. What of those who are not in the "normal" or "average" range?—above average, below average, borderline defective, superior, mentally defective, very superior. If one is not average, one must be something else.

Educational testing has made its greatest contribution in describing to what degree children depart from the average. To illustrate this point, consider Lefty, Freddy, Gunther, Nancy, and Jane, who were each asked 15 questions (e.g., What is a submarine? Who was Tutankhamen?). Their scores were 8, 6, 5, 7, and 4. Whether the degree to which these children are average will ever be determined is questionable, but we can calculate their average score on this test. This is accomplished by adding 8 + 6 + 5 + 7 + 4, finding the sum of these five scores (which is 30), and then dividing by the number of scores so that 30 divided by 5 is 6. The mean, or average score, is 6.

Most students do not willingly take a statistics course; most students claim an aversion for statistics. This may be the result of boring instructors, uninteresting textbooks, courses that fail to meet student needs, forcing students to memorize countless formulae that will quickly be forgotten, the tedium and exactitude of mathematics, or a combination of these or other factors. For those of you who approach numbers with trepidation, fear not an outpouring of symbols, formulae, and inexplicable combinations of numbers. However, several concepts will facilitate our pursuit of the "average" child. As an example, the average score of a test can be described as

$$\frac{\Sigma X}{N}$$

where the symbol Σ can be read as "find the sum of all," the symbol X designates the test scores from which the mean will be found, and N indicates the number of test scores. The mean can be reported in various ways ranging from the verbal (the mean is 39.6), to the symbolic ($M = 39.6$ or $\overline{X} = 39.6$).

In the example involving Lefty and his friends, where the mean was found to be exactly 6.0, we can state accurately that two children were below the mean, one child was at the mean, and two children were above the mean. However, because a child is below the mean does not mean that he (the child) is below average. If a child received an IQ score of 99 and the mean IQ was 100, we would be accurate in saying that a score of 99 was below the mean. However we would be remiss in saying that a score of 99 was below average, since "below average" suggests that a child is somehow deficient.

The essential question is not so much whether a child is above or below the mean, but rather how far a child's test score is above or below the mean. If the mean is 6 and a child received a score of 8, we know that his score is two points above the mean

$$X - \overline{X} = \text{POINTS FROM THE MEAN}$$

or

$$8 - 6 = 2,$$

but what does two points above the mean signify? Would two points above the mean in this instance be the same as two points above the mean if the mean was 500 and the score was 498?

What is needed to understand how scores vary around the mean, and to interpret what a single score denotes, is an index. Enter the standard deviation. This index can be designated by s, SD, S or a small Greek sigma (σ). Table VI illustrates how a standard deviation is found. First, the mean is determined. Second, the mean is subtracted from each score. These results show how many raw score points each person deviates from the mean. As an example, Louie received a raw score of 4. The mean subtracted from a score of four results in -2. This means that Louie was two points below the mean. Third, the number of points a score deviates from the mean is squared. If this is not done and the deviations from the mean are added ($+2 + 0 + -1 + +1 + -2$), the sum will always be 0. Fourth, the squared deviations from the mean are summed. In Table VI the sum of the squared deviations from the mean is $+10$. Fifth, the sum of the squared deviations from the mean is divided by the number of children, or $10 / 5 = 2$. Dividing the sum of the squared deviations from the mean by the number of children results in what is called the variance.* The variance can be symbolized by s^2, SD^2, or by σ^2. Sixth, the standard deviation is found by finding the square root of the variance; or, stated another way, the standard deviation is found by dividing the sum of the squared deviations by the number of

---

* If a set of scores is intended to represent a sample from a large set of scores, dividing $\Sigma (X - \overline{X})^2$ by N will tend to underestimate the variance of the larger population. This underestimate can be compensated for by dividing $\Sigma (X - \overline{X})^2$ by N $- 1$.

children (10/5=2) and then finding the square root. The square root of 2 can be symbolized by

$$\sqrt{2}$$

and the answer is 1.414. The standard deviation for scores 8, 6, 5, 7, and 4 is 1.414.

TABLE VI

CALCULATION OF STANDARD DEVIATION USING
DEVIATION FROM MEAN METHOD

Child	Score (X)	(—)	$(\overline{X})$	Deviation from Mean $(X - \overline{X})$	Squared Deviation $(X - \overline{X})^2$
Mary	8	—	6	+2	+4
Fred	6	—	6	0	0
Herman	5	—	6	−1	+1
Jane	7	—	6	+1	+1
Louie	4	—	6	−2	+4
Sums	30				+10

ΣX (Sum of Scores) = 30

X (Mean) = $\dfrac{30}{5}$ = 6

$\Sigma(X - X)^2$ (Sum of Squared Deviations from Mean) = +10

standard deviation   *(SD)*

$$SD = \sqrt{\frac{\Sigma(X - \overline{X})^2}{N}}$$

$$SD = \sqrt{\frac{10}{5}}$$

$$SD = \sqrt{2}$$

$$SD = 1.4142$$

Determining the standard deviation by using the actual deviations from the mean is conceptually useful but computationally impractical. If the mean is 234.592 and there are a large number of raw scores, subtracting the mean from each score would be a nerve-racking task.

Fortunately, there is an easier method for calculating the standard deviation than battling a long list of unwieldy deviations from the mean. This simplified method is shown in Table VII and entails finding only one new quantity:

$$\Sigma X^2$$

This new quantity is the sum of squared raw scores. As shown in Table VII, the first step is to square each raw score. Second, the sum of these squared raw scores is found ($\Sigma X^2 = 190$). Third, ΣX^2 is divided by the number of children, or 5. This results in a value of 38. Fourth, the mean (which is 6) is squared ($6^2 = 36$). Fifth, the squared mean (36) is subtracted from ΣX^2 so that $38 - 36 = 2$. As in the first example, 2 is the variance, and the standard deviation is found by finding the square root of 2, which is, as it will always be, 1.414.

The advent of computers and the wonderfully versatile hand calculator has made the calculation of the mean and the standard deviation a minor task. If you do not have a liking for computer centers or the glow of hand calculators, there is an abundance of persons available who can calculate (and some who even strangely enjoy) statistics. Although the calculation of the mean and standard deviation is no longer a burdensome task, you should be aware of how these statistics are found. One cannot deal with abuses if one does not have the vaguest idea of what is being abused.

The scores are recorded, the calculations over, and now the matter of interpretation. Consider a test on which the mean is 6, the standard deviation 1.414, and a child received a score of 8, we can determine how many standard deviations this score is above or below the mean by subtracting the mean from each score and dividing by the standard deviation or

$$\frac{\text{SCORE} - \text{MEAN}}{\text{STANDARD DEVIATION}}$$

Thus, $8 - 6 = 2$, and divided by $1.414 = 1.414$. This child's score is 1.414 standard deviations above the mean. A child with

TABLE VII

CALCULATION OF STANDARD DEVIATION USING RAW SCORE METHOD

Child	Score (X)	Square Each Score (X²)
Mary	8	64
Fred	6	36
Herman	5	25
Jane	7	49
Louie	4	16
Sums	30	190

$\Sigma X = 30$

$\overline{X} = \dfrac{30}{5} = 6$

ΣX^2 (Sum of All Squared Scores) $= 190$

$$SD = \sqrt{\frac{\Sigma X^2}{N} - \overline{X}^2}$$

$$SD = \sqrt{\frac{190}{5} - 6^2}$$

$$SD = \sqrt{38 - 36}$$

$$SD = \sqrt{2}$$

$$SD = 1.4142$$

a score of 5 is .707 standard deviations below the mean or 5 − 6 = −1, and −1 divided by 1.414 = −.707. A child with a score of 6 would be 0.0 standard deviations below the mean; that is to say, his score would be right at the mean since 6 − 6 = 0, and 0 divided by 1.414 = 0.

In this example, a score two points above or below the mean would be 1.414 standard deviations away from the mean. What if the mean was 500 and the standard deviation was 100. Would a score of 498, which is two points below a mean of 500, also be 1.414 standard deviations away from the mean? No. A score of 498 is two points below the mean of 500 (498 − 500 = −2), but −2 divided by 100 (the standard deviation) is −.02. Therefore, when the mean is 6 and the standard deviation is 1.414, a score two points below the mean is more standard deviations below the mean than when the mean is 500 and the standard deviation is 100.

The mean and standard deviation are of vital importance to educational testing because they provide a basis for interpreting and comparing scores. (Remember, however, not to confuse what is important for testing with what is important for a child.) If a child received a score of 10 on a test which had a mean of 6 and a standard deviation of 1.414, what would this score be comparable to if the mean was 100 and the standard deviation was 15? First of all, a score of 10 would be 2.829 standard deviations above a mean of 6, since 10 − 6 = 4, and 4 divided by 1.414 = 2.829. Now, what is 2.829 standard deviations above a mean of 100 when the standard deviation is 15? This can be found by multiplying 15 by 2.829 (the answer is 42.435) and then adding this product to 100. The answer is 142.435. Where else but in educational testing could a score of 10 be comparable to a score of 142.435?

NORMAL CURVE

A normal curve would seem, for one reason or another, a promising idea for defining a normal child. A normal curve will certainly assist in our interpretation of scores, means, and standard deviations; unfortunately a normal curve will not lead us to the ethereal normal child.

The normal curve is a mathematical construct, a mathematical function (a mathematician's dream of reality would be too strong) showing how scores are distributed. The scores shown in Table VIII illustrate the concept underlying the normal curve. Most children score around the mean; fewer scores are found as you move away from the mean; and the least number of scores occur at the very highest and very lowest ranges. There are 100 scores recorded in Table VIII. The majority of scores center about the mean (which is 4.5), while the scores become less frequent at the higher and lower extremes. As an example, there are 34 scores of 4 and 5, but only 4 scores of 0 and 9.

TABLE VIII

EXAMPLE OF NORMAL FREQUENCY DISTRIBUTION

Raw Score	Frequency
9	2
8	5
7	9
6	15
5	19
4	19
3	15
2	9
1	5
0	2

To better illustrate the concept of a normal curve, the scores and frequencies shown in Table VIII were plotted in Figure 4. When the points are connected by a solid line, a portrait of the normal curve emerges. As was indicated before, the normal curve is a mathematical concept, or a visual depiction of that concept. Reality and the normal curve are not the same. The normal curve specifically states that 34.13 percent of the scores will fall between the mean and one standard deviation above the mean; 13.59 percent of the cases will fall between one standard deviation above the mean and two standard deviations above the mean; and 2.15 percent of the scores will fall between two standard deviations above the mean and three standard deviations above the mean. Likewise, the same percentages will occur below the mean.

The curve shown in Figure 4 lacks the exactness of the mathematical normal curve, but one would be justified in saying that the scores were normally distributed. The mean of the data shown in Figure 4 is 4.5 and the standard deviation is 1.98. As is shown, one standard deviation above the mean (or one 1.98) is a score of 6.48 (4.5 + 1.98). Exactly 34 percent of the scores shown in Figure 4 occurred between the mean (4.5) and a score of 6.48. This is a little short of 34.13, but a reasonable facsimile. Going on, 14 percent of the scores in Figure 4 occurred

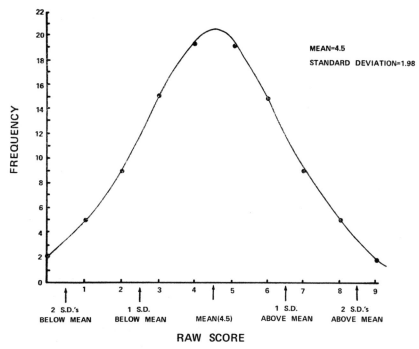

Figure 4.   An example of a *normal* curve.

between one standard deviation above the mean (6.48) and two
standard deviations above the mean (8.46). Finally, 2 percent
of the scores shown in Figure 4 were in excess of two standard
deviations above the mean. In actuality the normal curve is
infinite; that is, all scores do not occur within two or three
standard deviations. Scores can occur 5 standard deviations
above the mean or 10 standard deviations above the mean. However, a score 10 standard deviations above the mean will occur
very, very infrequently.

Lest you be misled by the symmetry and exactness of the
normal curve, Figure 5 illustrates the type of distribution one
might find upon administering a test to a group of children.
This does not mean that scores cannot be "something like" a
normal curve, but only that any and all types of score distributions can occur and that the bell-shaped appearance of a normal
curve will not always appear.

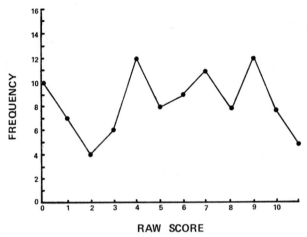

Figure 5.   A frequency distribution that is not especially *normal*.

The mean and standard deviation are the essence for evaluating many test scores. This is accomplished by determining how many standard deivations a child's score is above or below the mean. But so what if a score is two standard deviations below the mean or 1.64 standard deviations above the mean? Scoring above or below the mean in terms of standard deviations has very little meaning on the surface. Alas, this is where the concept of a normal curve proves useful. Since the mathematical normal curve is so exact (34.13% of the scores will occur between the mean and one standard deviation above the mean), we can exactly state the percent of scores that will occur below or above any given point. As an example, if 50 percent of the scores occur below the mean and 34.13 percent of the scores occur between the mean and one standard deviation above the mean, then 84.13 percent of the scores (50% + 34.13 % = 84.13%) must occur below one standard deviation above the mean. Does this have a ring of percentile ranks?—the percent of cases above or below a specific score. Yes, indeed! Using the mathematical normal curve, there is a relationship between standard deviations above or below the mean and percentile ranks. Table IX illustrates this basic relationship by showing the number of standard deviations above or below the mean and the corresponding percentile rank (*sans* decimal places to the hundredth). Keeping this relationship in mind, a person could say that 0.0 standard deviations above the mean is equivalent to a percentile rank of 50; one standard deviation above the mean is equivalent to a percentile rank of 84; and that two standard deviations below the mean is equivalent to a percentile rank of 2.

TABLE IX

RELATIONSHIP BETWEEN NUMBER OF STANDARD DEVIATIONS
BELOW AND ABOVE THE MEAN AND PERCENTILE RANKS
USING THE NORMAL CURVE

Number of Standard Deviations Above or Below the Mean	*Percentile Rank*
+2.5	99
+2.0	98
+1.5	93
+1.0	84
+0.5	69
0.0	50
—0.5	31
—1.0	16
—1.5	7
—2.0	2
—2.5	1

The great advantage of using the mean and standard deviation to interpret a child's score is that the distance between raw scores in terms of standard deviations will be the same across the scale. As you will remember, differences between scores resulted in unequal percentile rank differences. However, if the standard deviation of a test is 8, the difference between a score of 0 and 4 will be 0.5 standard deviations, and the difference between scores of 24 and 28 will also be 0.5 standard deviations. You might not regard this finding as earthshaking or cause for celebration, but statisticians find solace in knowing that numbers can be added and subtracted without fretting over whether the differences between points are equal or not. Part of educational statistics is not so much what the scores mean, but that the computations are correct.

As useful and logical as the relation between standard deviations above and below the mean and percentile ranks might be, reality is not always so kind as to approximate the normal curve.

Table X illustrates a score distribution where the relationship between standard deviations from the mean and percentile ranks is far from being perfect. The scores on this test range between 0 and 20. Ten children received the very lowest score (0), then the scores appear to form a distribution around a score of 3. The large number of 0 scores could be attributed to a lack of interest, not understanding the test instructions, or not understanding the test task. Whatever the cause, a distribution such as this would indicate that the occurrence of a large number of 0 scores needed further investigation. In addition to the unusual frequencies at the lower score range, the distribution of scores shown in Table X is also skewed to the right or positively skewed. This could be the result of either the 100 children sampled, or the test. If it were the result of the sample, testing a different 100 children would tend to eliminate much of the skewness. However, the type of distribution shown in Table X is most likely to occur when test items are too difficult.

TABLE X

RELATIONSHIP BETWEEN STANDARD DEVIATIONS (*SD*) AND
PERCENTILE RANKS FOR AN ASYMMETRICAL DISTRIBUTION

Raw Score	Frequency	SDs from Mean*	Percentile Rank
20	1	+2.72	99
19	1	+2.54	97
18	1	+2.36	95
17	1	+2.18	93
16	1	+2.00	91
15	1	+1.82	89
14	0	+1.63	88
13	1	+1.45	87
12	0	+1.27	86
11	1	+1.09	85
10	2	+0.91	82
9	0	+0.73	80
8	1	+0.5	79
7	1	+0.36	77
6	2	+0.18	74
5	2	+0.00	70
4	4	—0.18	64
3	10	—0.36	50
2	8	—0.5	32
1	2	—0.73	22
0	10	—0.91	10

* The mean score is 5.00 and the standard deviation is 5.51.

After the blissful symmetry of the normal curve, where relationships are predictable and exact, the distribution shown in Table X is somewhat chaotic. The mean of these scores is 5.0, but the 50th percentile is a score of 3. A normal distribution yields equivalent means and medians. In this example the mean is two points higher than the median. Likewise, in a normal sample one would find that a score two standard deviations above the mean was equivalent to a percentile rank of 98. In this sample, however, a score two standard deviations above the mean (a raw score of 16) is equivalent to a percentile rank of 91.

The normal curve is mathematically elegant and provides a useful frame of reference for interpreting scores. However, normal curve and reality are not synonymous, and a distribution that seriously departs from normality can affect the interpretation of a child's test performance. In Table X a score of 0 is equivalent to 0.91 standard deviations below the mean. In a normal curve, 0.91 standard deviations would indicate that approximately 18 percent of scores were below that point. However, in this example a score of 0 is equivalent to a percentile rank of 10. Because of the nature of this distribution, interpreting a raw score of 0, or any other raw score, is a difficult task.

THE GREAT SCORE PUZZLE

One of the great innovations that has given an element of variety to educational testing is the ability to transform scores. This does not mean that scores are tampered with or that a child's test score can be recklessly disfigured. On the contrary, scores are transformed with the ostensible purpose of clarifying, and not muddling, the interpretation of a child's test performance. Nonetheless, transformed scores can be deceptive insomuch as such scores can produce indices clothed with meaning that is more fiction than fact.

The basis of transforming scores lies first with determining how many standard deviations a child's score is above or below the mean. The number of standard deviations a child's score is above or below the mean is often referred to as a z score or a standard score. As an example, on a test that had a mean of 39 and a standard deviation of 5, a child with a raw score of 44 would have a z score of +1.0. This is the same as saying that this child had a score that was one standard deviation above the mean. The method for finding the number of standard deviations a child scores above or below the mean is the same as previously described:

$$z \text{ score or } \frac{\text{standard}}{\text{score}} \text{ or } \frac{SDs \text{ above or}}{\text{below mean}} = \frac{\text{SCORE} - \text{MEAN}}{\text{STANDARD DEVIATION}}$$

The rationale for using z scores or standard scores is appealing. Reporting a raw score can be meaningless. After all, what does a score of 4 signify? Or a score of 45? Or a raw score of 947? Instead of reporting raw scores, simply state how many standard deviations a child's score is above or below the mean. In other words, only report a z score. If we know that a child has a z score of 0.0, he has a raw score that is at the mean. We might not know what the actual mean of the test was, but we do know that a z score of 0.0 is at the mean. Similarly, a z score of −1.5 indicates that a child was 1.5 standard deviations below the mean. We might not know what the actual raw score was, but we do know that a z score of −1.5 is 1.5 standard deviations below the mean. If we further assume that the distribution is approximately normal, we might also infer that a score 1.5 standard deviations below the mean is equivalent to a percentile rank of 7 (see Table IX).

The magic of standard scores is that it makes no difference how the scores are reported as long as a score indicates how many standard deviations a child's score is above or below the mean.

You will recall Doctor K's development of percentile rank norms. Assume now that the doctor received word from his publisher that a standard score would enhance the interpretability and salability of his test. Doctor K takes the not-so-subtle hint and immediately calculates the mean and standard deviation for the 25 children he tested (see scores shown in Table III). He finds the mean to be 2.0 and the standard deviation to be 0.894. He then finds that a score of 4 is 2.24 standard deviations above the mean, a score of 3 is 1.12 standard deviations above the mean, a score of 2 is at the mean (so a score of 2 has a z score of 0.0), a score of 1 is 1.12 standard deviations below the mean, and a score of 0 is 2.24 standard deviations below the mean.

Doctor K sends this information, z scores and corresponding raw scores, to his publisher. His publisher responds by saying that Doctor K is demented and that no one would understand what a z score meant. After all, how often will a parent receive a list of a child's z scores?

Doctor K, in spite of ruffled feelings, decides that his publisher is right and that he needs a device that will simplify the interpretation of raw scores. He discusses his problem with several friends, inspects several tests, and comes to the conclusion that he should be using stanine scores. Stanine is a contraction of "standard nine." Stanine scores can range between 1 and 9, and the mean stanine is 5 and the standard deviation is 2. Doctor K selected stanines because they are frequently used with educational tests (especially achievement tests), they are not as messy as z scores (a stanine of 7 seems so much simpler than a corresponding z score of $+1.00$), and they are easily recorded.

If you are confused about the relationship between z scores and stanines, you shouldn't be. Remember that the purpose of using standard scores is to report the number of standard deviations a child is above or below the mean. If we know the mean of a distribution is 5 and the standard deviation is 2, and a child received a score of 7, then his score is $+1.00$ standard deviations above a mean of 5. Furthermore, we need not restrict ourselves to stanines. We could just as easily say that the mean of the distribution is 500 and the standard deviation is 100, and a child who is $+1.00$ standard deviations above the mean (or a child with a z score of $+1.00$) has a score equivalent to 600; this is so since 600 is $+1.00$ standard deviations above a score of 500.

Doctor K converts the five z scores for his test using the following transformation:

$$z \text{ score} \times \begin{matrix} \text{DESIRED} \\ \text{STANDARD} \\ \text{DEVIATION} \end{matrix} + \begin{matrix} \text{DESIRED} \\ \text{MEAN} \end{matrix} = \begin{matrix} \text{NEW} \\ \text{STANDARD} \\ \text{SCORE} \end{matrix}$$

So, for a child who received a score $+2.24$ standard deviations above the mean (or a z score of $+2.24$), the equivalent stanine score would be:

$$+2.24 \times 2 + 5 = 9.48$$

Since stanines range between 1 and 9 and decimals are not used, this score is rounded off to 9. A raw score of 3, which is $+1.12$ standard deviations above the mean, is equivalent to a stanine of 7 ($+1.12 \times 2 + 5 = 7.24$). A child with a score of 2 (z score $= 0.00$) would have a stanine of 5 ($0.00 \times 2 + 5 = 5$). A child with a raw score of 1 (z score $= -1.12$) would have a stanine of 3 ($-1.12 \times 2 + 5 = 2.76$). Finally, a child with a raw score of 0 (z score $= -2.24$) would have a stanine of 1 ($-2.24 \times 2 + 5 = 0.52$).

If you are wondering why someone decided that the mean stanine should be 5 and the standard deviation should be 2, the decision is completely arbitrary; that is, the selection of the mean and standard deviation is more a cosmetic decision than a useful one. What is important is that we are able to state how many standard deviations a child's score is above or below the mean. If Doctor K wished to market his test as an IQ test, he might have selected a mean of 100 and a standard deviation of 15. If this mean and standard deviation were chosen, a z score of $+2.24$ would be equivalent to an IQ-type score of 134 ($+2.24 \times 15 + 100 = 133.60$). Likewise, a z score of -1.12 would be equivalent to an IQ-type score of 83 ($-1.12 \times 15 + 100 = 83.2$).

Although the mean and standard deviation selected are arbitrary with respect to interpreting scores, certain means and standard deviations have been used to convey specific types of information. Table XI presents several of the more popular means and standard deviations. The first column presents z scores where the mean is 0.0 and the standard deviation is 1.0. These scores are commonly used by researchers or those persons satisfied with knowing how many standard deviations a child's score is above or below the mean with the least amount of masquerade. The columns showing means of 100 and standard deviations of 16 and 15 have been customarily associated with IQ scores. The mean of 500 and standard deviation of 100 are frequently used with college entrance tests and examinations for professional schools. The mean of 50 and standard deviation of 10 are often suggested by statisticians but have nonetheless remained relatively unpopular in educational testing circles. The mean of 5 and standard deviation of 2 (stanines) have been used with a variety of tests but appear to be especially popular with achievement tests. The mean of 10 and standard deviation of 3 are used with subtests of the Wechsler Intelligence Scale for Children—Revised (Wechsler, 1974). The mean of 36 and standard deviation of 6 were selected by the authors of the Illinois Test of Psycholinguistic Abilities (Kirk, McCarthy, and Kirk, 1968) and were apparently selected so as "to guard against the direct comparison of the ITPA scaled scores derived from samples of *average* children" (Paraskevopoulous and Kirk, 1969, p. 85).

Standard scores provide a useful means of interpreting a child's test performance. All too often, however, standard scores are used in a perfunctory fashion without due regard for a child's skill, ability, or potential. If the standard deviation on a test was small, a few raw score points would result in a large departure, in terms of standard deviations, from the mean.

TABLE XI

THE GREAT SCORE PUZZLE

Mean =	0.0	100	100	500	50	5	10	36
SD =	1.0	16	15	100	10	2	3	6
	+2.5	140	138	750	75		18	51
	+2.0	132	130	700	70	9	16	48
	+1.5	124	123	650	65	8	15	45
	+1.0	116	115	600	60	7	13	42
	+0.5	108	108	550	55	6	12	39
	+0.0	100	100	500	50	5	10	36
	—0.5	92	93	450	45	4	9	33
	—1.0	84	85	400	40	3	7	30
	—1.5	76	78	350	35	2	6	27
	—2.0	68	70	300	30	1	4	24
	—2.5	60	63	250	25		3	21

Furthermore, setting the mean and standard deviation to have specific values does not make the resulting standard score any more valid or beneficial. To say that a child has an IQ of 85 on a test with a mean of 100 and a standard deviation of 15 is no more useful than the economical statement that a child was one standard deviation below the mean. Finally, standard scores are not niches of truth and perfection. Standard scores are affected, and occasionally drastically, by inadequate samples, inadequate sampling, bizarre score distributions, and inherently bad tests. Standard scores often imply an accuracy and usefulness which is little more than a figment of a test developer's imagination. Knowing that a child is above or below average on a single test does not negate the fundamental responsibility of knowing the child.

Chapter Four

THE MYSTIFYING IQ

IQ TESTS

MANY PARENTS, TEACHERS, and test specialists dislike IQ tests. Opinions regarding IQ tests range from "a silly nuisance" to "noxious, unctuous numbers which degrade human dignity." The dissatisfaction over tests of intelligence emanates from the stigmatizing effect that a low IQ can have, callous misuse of IQ tests and scores, and the naivete involved in attempting to portray the intellectual complexity of an individual by a single score.

Even after first being introduced, the use of an index to represent intelligence did not enjoy overwhelming enthusiasm. Ebel (1964) reported that after the German psychologist Wilhelm Stern became aware of how the intelligence quotient that he introduced (circa 1912) was being overgeneralized, he "charged one of his students coming to America to 'kill the IQ.'" The degree to which such a sinister plot (albeit interesting) had existed during the fledgling days of educational testing is questionable. Stern (1938), however, did state that "to base any pedagogical estimate upon the IQ alone for practical purposes (e.g., for assignment to opportunity classes), is indefensible" (pp. 310-311).

Past animosity or present hostility does not belie the widespread use of IQ tests and IQ scores. One of the great fallacies concerning IQ scores is that each individual has "an IQ." The implication is that somehow, somewhere one number—beyond reproach and criticism, and deathly accurate—can be assigned to each individual. A person unfamiliar with IQ tests does not think of a multitude of IQ tests, a seemingly endless number of tasks, or that an IQ is only a score, but that one index, one quotient, a single number is sufficient to describe a person's intellectual development and potential.

There is no such thing as *a person's IQ*. This is a myth. A person's reported IQ score is nothing more than a score on a test—an index as to how an individual performs on a task or series of tasks in comparison to a specific reference group.

There is no one method for determining a person's intelligence. As a matter of fact, there is not necessarily one type of intelligence that can be measured. An IQ test, in contrast to the austere finality of an IQ score, does not entail a microscopic examination of cerebral processing. The brain is not weighed, the brain is not seen, and little more than a small sampling of behavior is used to pronounce a child's intelligence. An IQ test might consist of nothing more than a series of questions (e.g., What is a hammer? How many days are there in a week? Who is the president of the United States? Why do we need firemen?). But this does not mean that intelligence is limited to a series of verbal responses. One could argue that there is a social intelligence, a creative intelligence, or a concrete intelligence; one could say that intelligence involves adapting, abstracting, verbalizing, adjusting, analyzing, synthesizing, surviving, enduring, and an infinity of known and unknown traits, abilities, and skills.

An IQ test, as one might rightly suspect, measures *test intelligence*. A child is asked questions, given a test form to complete, or required to perform in some other way. However, even with test intelligence there is no standard testing procedure or technique. Probably the best that can be done with respect to classifying IQ tests and IQ test tasks (a real tongue twister) is to say that there are verbal tests and tasks and nonverbal tests and tasks. The difference between a test and task is very important. A test might involve several different tasks (e.g., counting beads, answering questions, completing puzzles), but a task will generally differ only in terms of item difficulty; that is, each item of a task will be increasingly more difficult (e.g., repeat the digits 3-1-8, then repeat 6-4-2-5, then repeat 4-9-3-2-7-1).

Verbal tasks include basic vocabulary questions (e.g., What is a glass?), naming objects (e.g., Examiner presents child with pencil and asks, "What is this?"), information (e.g., When is Christmas?), verbal associations (e.g., In what way are a table and chair alike?), verbal understanding (e.g., Why do we have automobiles?), verbal arithmetic problems (e.g., If you had two apples and were given three more, how many would you have altogether?), auditory memory (e.g., Repeat the following digits: 5-2-7-4), and general verbal comprehension (e.g., A bicycle was turned over and a boy was holding his head. What had happened?).

There are really no restrictions on the type (e.g., information, associations) or form (e.g., single-word answers, multiple-choice questions, verbal descriptions) of questions that can be asked when constructing an intelligence test. The only factor limiting the test is the imagination of the test developer.

Verbal tasks are popular because they are easily constructed, easily administered, and discriminate between children on the basis of verbal ability. A child with high verbal ability is said to have high intelligence, while a child with low verbal ability is said to have low intelligence. Needless to say, children who come from homes where ideas, words, and concepts float about freely will, more often than not, score higher on IQ tests than children who come from homes where verbal interaction is at a premium. For that matter, one might postulate that children who come from homes similar to those who selected the verbal test items will perform better than children who do not come from such homes. The assessment of intelligence is plagued by a goodly number of complicating factors. However, the practice of remaining aloof from these factors greatly enhances the *perceived* usefulness and ethos of IQ scores.

Unlike verbal tasks, performance tasks usually center around a nonverbal stimulus (e.g., blocks, a picture, a puzzle). A child might be requested to draw a picture of a man (or woman, or himself), arrange blocks according to a previously shown pattern, put together a puzzle, find a missing element in a picture (e.g., a picture of a horse with no tail), sequence a series of pictures so that they form a story, copy designs, coding (e.g., 1=T, 8=S, 3=L; then 8=__, 3=__, 1=__), stringing beads, differentiating between circles and squares, and matching geometric shapes.

Figure 6 presents three commonly used nonverbal tasks. The first task is maze performance. A child traces a line to the small house in the center of the maze. Apparently, what is good for a mouse is good for a child. The second item involves copying geometric shapes. The shapes are presented according to their developmental difficulty ranging from a preschool task (copying a circle) to a school age task (copying a diamond). The last task requires a child to count the total number of cubes. This task, when the configuration of cubes is complex, is one of the more aggravating tasks in educational testing.

Although verbal and nonverbal tasks are often seen as a dichotomy, the distinction between these areas is not always clear. A verbal task might involve nonverbal elements (e.g.,

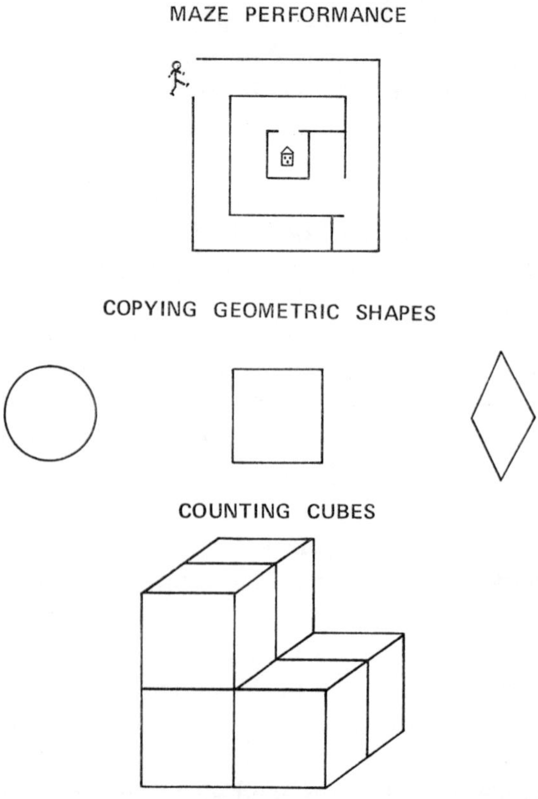

MAZE PERFORMANCE

COPYING GEOMETRIC SHAPES

COUNTING CUBES

Figure 6.   Several *nonverbal* or *performance* tasks.

objects, pictures), while nonverbal tests are usually preceded by verbal instructions as well as often requiring a verbal response on the part of a child. In addition, even a nonverbal task such as counting cubes does not completely ignore the question of varying verbal ability and that a child with superior verbal skills cannot use those skills to better solve nonverbal problems.

There are numerous ways in which IQ tests can be classified. Categorizing tests on the basis of verbal or nonverbal emphasis is one method, differentiating between tests on the basis of the tasks involved is another, while grouping tests as being either individual tests of intelligence or group tests of intelligence is still another method. An individual test of intelligence, as the name implies, requires that a test be administered to a child in a one-to-one situation. An individual test of intelligence might involve a single task (e.g., a vocabulary-type task) or incorporate ten or more tasks. Testing time can vary between several minutes and several hours. Likewise, the quality of individual tests of intelligence will vary between "awful by any standard" and "good from a test construction standpoint." Individual tests of intelligence are generally more (much more) expensive than group tests of intelligence, although the relation between cost, amount of testing time, and quality is probably low at best.

Group tests of intelligence are administered to groups of children, young adults, and adults. Overall, group tests are bad. Many school administrators select group tests because they are inexpensive, they can be given to large numbers of individuals in a short period of time, and they yield an IQ; after all, an IQ is an IQ! Of all the criticisms that can be leveled at IQ tests, one would like to believe that individual tests allow an examiner to use his perspicacity, his understanding of a child, and the situation to better learn what a child can and cannot do. Group tests, on the other hand, are little more than paper-pencil tests, often involving reading and often of the multiple choice variety, which produce a score at the expense of individual understanding.

IQ SCORES

We have already discussed the most commonly used method for determining IQ scores. A child is given a test, a raw score determined, and the number of standard deviations this score is above or below the mean calculated. Assume that a child is given a series of verbal analogies to complete (e.g., Pen is to paper as table is to————.). Her final raw score on this test is found to be 17; that is, 17 analogies were correctly completed. Prior to this time, the test was standardized on a group of 200 children similar in age to the girl who was recently tested. The mean score of the standardization or normative group was found to be 20, and the standard deviation was found to be 3. Included with the test (in the test manual) are norms that show that a child who receives a raw score of 17 for the age specified has an IQ of 85.

Test manuals rarely require an individual to determine how many standard deviations a child is above or below the mean. This task is undertaken by the test developer and included in the test manual. However, having a raw score, mean, and standard deviation, and then determining an IQ is an easy matter. A raw score of 17 is exactly one standard deviation below the mean ($17 - 20 = -3$, and -3 divided by $3 = -1$). Now, if the mean of a distribution is 100 and the standard deviation is 15, one standard deviation below the mean would be equivalent to a score of 85. This can be found by: $-1 \times 15 + 100 = 85$.

The above method, currently the fashion in testing for calculating IQ scores, is a far cry from the original concept of IQ. An IQ was originally intended to indicate a quotient, a ratio between mental age and chronological age. This ratio is expressed by the following formula:

$$IQ = \frac{MA}{CA} \, (100)$$

MA indicates mental age, and CA signifies chronological age. As MA increases, the resulting quotient (IQ) increases, and as CA increases, the resulting quotient decreases. As an example, if a child was found to have an MA of 8 years and he was 10 years old, he would have a corresponding IQ of 80: 8 divided by $10 = .8$, and $.8 \times 100 = 80$. If a second child was found to have an MA of 5 years and he was 5 years old, the resulting IQ would be 100. Finally, if a child was found to have an MA of 6 years and 6 months and a chronological age of 5 years and

3 months, the resulting IQ would be 124. In this example MA and CA were first converted to months so that 6 years 6 months is equal to 78 months and 5 years 3 months is equal to 63 months. The IQ was then calculated using the traditional formula: 78 divided by 63 = 1.238, and 1.238 × 100 = 124 (rounded).

The primary task involved in determining IQ using the traditional intelligence quotient formula is first determining a child's MA. Table XII demonstrates how an MA is found. Here, four age levels are shown. Six tasks were assigned to each age level. Assume that items were assigned to an age level if, and depending on several additional factors, approximately 50 to 75 percent of the children at a specific age level in the normative group passed that particular item. The sample shown in Table XII shows that the child tested passed all items at the 5-year-old level. This signifies that this child's basal age is 5 years. The basal age indicates that a child will receive credit for all items beneath that point, even though these items were never actually administered.

At the 6-year-old level the child passed the following items: arithmetic concepts, block design, analogies, and descriptions. The difficulty of the descriptions task at age level 6 was, of course, more difficult than the descriptions task at age level 5. Since 4 items were passed, this child was credited with an additional 8 months credit. As can be seen, with 6 items at each age level, 12 months credit would be given if all items were passed. At age level 7, one item was passed (digit span) and 2 more months credit was given. Last, at age level 8 all items were failed. This is the ceiling level, which means that tasks at the upper age levels are not administered.

This child's MA is found by adding all credit received: 5 years plus 8 months for age level 6 plus 2 months for age level 7 for a total of 5 years and 10 months. If this child was 5 years old, the calculated IQ would be 117 (70 months divided by 60 months = 1.17, and 1.17 × 100 = 117).

As pleasant as the idea of MA might seem, the calculation of intelligence quotients has several serious limitations. First, no one would really believe that an 11-year-old child with an MA of 8 would function at the same cognitive level as a 5-year-old child with an MA of 8. School achievement, social development, and general cognitive experiences alone would dictate vast

TABLE XII

AN EXAMPLE SHOWING THE CALCULATION OF A
CHILD'S MENTAL AGE (MA) SCORE

Age Level	Task	Pass	Credit	Total[*] Credit
	Vocabulary	Yes	2 months	
	Mazes	Yes	2 months	
	Incomplete Pictures	Yes	2 months	5
5	Digit Span	Yes	2 months	Years
	Counting	Yes	2 months	
	Descriptions	Yes	2 months	
	.... Basal Age			
	Arithmetic Concepts	Yes	2 months	
	Block Design	Yes	2 months	
6	Copying	No	none	8
	Analogies	Yes	2 months	Months
	Incomplete Pictures	No	none	
	Descriptions	Yes	2 months	
	Definitions	No	none	
	Similarities	No	none	
7	Digit Span	Yes	2 months	2
	Analogies	No	none	Months
	Identifying Pictures	No	none	
	Definitions	No	none	
	Memory	No	none	
	Vocabulary	No	none	
8	Block Design	No	none	
	Similarities	No	none	None
	Definitions	No	none	
	Comprehension	No	none	
	.... Ceiling Age			

[*] MA = 5 Years + 8 Months + 2 Months = 5 Years and 10 Months.

differences between two children having identical MAs but different chronological ages. Second, increases in MA result in different IQ increases for different age levels. A 4-year-old child with an MA of 6 would have an IQ of 150, but an 8-year-old child with an MA of 10 would have an IQ of 125. Third, using the traditional MA divided by CA quotient resulted in different IQ standard deviations for different age groups. Terman and Merrill (1937) reported IQ standard deviations ranging between 12.5 and 20.6. Thus, a child from an age group with a standard deviation of 20.6 who had an IQ of 79 would be one standard deviation below the mean, while a child from an age group where the standard deviation was 12.5 who had an IQ of 88 would also be one standard deviation below the mean. Statisticians and psychometricians might tolerate stigmatizing, misclassifying, or otherwise humiliating children by using IQ scores, but messy statistics would be sufficient cause for professional chastisement.

The demise of the traditional formula ($MA/CA \times 100 = IQ$) gave way to the standard deviation IQ. Remember, however, that IQ signifies Intelligence Quotient—the quotient of MA divided by CA. The standard deviation IQ is not really a quotient but, out of uncharacteristic sentimentality for traditional IQ ratios, virtually anything that deviates from a mean is wantonly labeled IQ. The gist of all this is that the intelligence quotient is not usually a quotient but a deviation score: thus, the IQ (a commemorative title) score (what an IQ is).

With the passing of the traditional IQ, the IQ score has had its ups and downs. Wechsler (1949) was not at all hesitant to lambaste the MA concept (a standard deviation IQ does not require finding a MA score) while at the same time touting the merits of the standard deviation IQ, which his test provided (Wechsler Intelligence Scale for Children). However, he then did a small turnabout by including a table to find MA equivalents in his test manual. Not to be outdone, the authors of the Stanford-Binet Intelligence Scale (Terman and Merrill, 1960), the counterpart of the Wechsler Intelligence Scale for Children, continued to incorporate the MA concept but adjusted the resulting IQs so that the mean was 100 and the standard deviation 16 for all age groups. This IQ, also called a deviation IQ, is not that dissimilar from Wechsler's standard deviation IQ. One has the feeling that educational testing is an endless circle.

Whatever the method for calculating IQ scores, it appears that the intelligence "quotient" is a thing of the past. In a way this is unfortunate, since one could always be secure in knowing that if two children received the same MA, a younger child would have a higher IQ than an older child. Intelligence quotients are like that. This, however, is not always the case with the newer IQ form. The Peabody Picture Vocabulary Test (Dunn, 1965) is an example. The task of this test entails saying a word and having a child point to the one of four illustrations that is best associated with that word. In all there are 150 items on this test, although in practice a child would not be given all items. If a 14-year-old child received a raw score of 58 (Form A), the corresponding IQ score would be 56. In contrast, if a child one year older (15) received the same raw score, he would be credited with having an IQ of 57! As can be seen, there are certain difficulties involved in interpreting an IQ score as an intelligence quotient.

IQ ABUSES

What positive remarks can be offered on behalf of IQ tests? Robinson and Robinson (1965), in a book entitled *The Mentally Retarded Child,* stated that IQ "tests have been very useful in helping to identify children who need special training, and they have been instrumental in establishing somewhat more orderly methods for admission procedures in institutions" (p. 389). They also cautioned that "there is little doubt that the IQ has been seriously misused because of persistent and erroneous notions about its permanence or magical powers to predict future performance" (p. 389).

Intelligence scores serve two basic purposes. First, IQs are used to comment on an individual's behavior, e.g. "No wonder. His IQ is 74." Or, "He's not doing bad work considering his IQ." Or, "She should be achieving at a much higher level considering her IQ." These comments will not help a child and will likely result in rigid attitudes and unrealistic expectations. Second, IQ scores are used to classify children for educational purposes. A major classification is educable mental retardation, which encompasses children with IQs approximately between 50 and 80. Those who use IQ scores extensively will be quick to add that IQ is not the only criterion for labeling a child educable mentally retarded; other criteria might include social adjustment, academic achievement, and learning ability. The fact remains, however, that IQ is often a primary reason (or excuse) for placing a child with other children who are said to be mentally retarded. Once a child is classified as being retarded the assumption is made that a program exists or that "special" experiences can be provided which are suitable for retarded children.

In the United States, the use of IQ to classify children as mentally retarded has been a complete and utter disaster. The very idea that a cutoff point exists, regardless of how many criteria are used to determine that point, which differentiates between retarded and nonretarded children, is preposterous. Wechsler (1974) cited IQs of 69 and below as belonging to the "mentally deficit" category. Does this mean that a child with an IQ of 70 is not retarded (borderline using Wechsler's terminology), and that a child with an IQ of 69 is? Many states legally require that a child have an IQ lower than a specified level (e.g., lower than 80) before assignment to a class of children said to be mentally retarded can be made. If the legal cutoff was 80, would one be morally justified in discriminating between normality and retardation on the basis of one IQ point? Moral justification or not, it is done, and the normality of a child often does hinge on something as meaningless as a single IQ point.

An IQ is only a score on a test. Misuse and misinterpretation of IQ scores occur when this fact is ignored. An IQ score is not a child's intelligence; an IQ score is not permanent; an IQ score explains nothing more than how one child performed on a task or series of tasks on one test. Ross, DeYoung, and Cohen (1971) discussed the case of *Diana v. State Board of Education* in northern California. The case involved nine Mexican-American children who came from homes where Spanish was the primary language and who were classified as being retarded on the basis of IQ testing conducted in the English language. What brave new insights are needed before the realization is made that children who have not had a life replete with English language experiences may have more than average difficulty with a test conducted in the English Language.

The use of IQ scores to classify children as mentally retarded is slanderous. To impugn a child's intellectual ability or potential on the basis of several responses is reprehensible. This psychometric name calling is tolerated only because of the defenselessness, the result of age rather than lack of spirit, of children. And for a child to learn that he is thought of by others as being "mentally retarded!" What must a child feel, what must a child think upon learning that he is perceived as being intellectually inferior?

The use of IQ scores to classify children as mentally retarded is often justified on the grounds that "mentally retarded" children need special training. There is no such thing as a mentally retarded child: every child has strengths, weaknesses, and every child needs special attention—"training" is one of those subtle derogatory terms reserved for children classified as retarded. When a child is categorized as mentally retarded, the subsequent placement typically provides an inferior curriculum, haphazard instruction, and ostracism from the mainstream of children. For this, this debasement of soul, spirit, and mind, we owe a very special debt to the principle of IQ.

Chapter Five

BUT THEY'RE EASY TO UNDERSTAND!

ACADEMIC ACHIEVEMENT

P_{AULA} S$_{CHNEIDER}$ is said to be achieving at the second grade level in arithmetic and at the fourth grade level in reading. If Paula were in the first grade, her teacher and parents might nod in commendation. If Paula were in the fifth grade, her performance would likely be the cause of deep concern.

Just as IQ is viewed as the quintessence of intellectual assessment, the level at which a child is said to achieve becomes the primary gauge of academic progress. If a child received a score of 3.4, we would say that in that particular subject achievement was equivalent to that of a child in the fourth month of the third grade. If a child received a raw score of 29 on a reading vocabulary test, and this was the median score for a group of children (the standardization group) in the eighth month of the second grade, this child would have a grade equivalent of 2.8.

Academic achievement, being the business of schools, is of special interest to those involved with educational testing. Academic achievement refers to what a child has been taught and to what a child has learned. A child is taught certain reading skills, and those skills taught are assessed; a child is taught arithmetic facts, and the degree to which those facts have been learned is measured; a child is presented with geographic information, and the extent to which that information has been acquired is assessed. The measurement of academic progress involves determining to what degree a child has acquired information presented or skills taught. Assessing the potential of a child to achieve is not within the realm of academic achievement, nor is assessing information or skills not yet taught.

The assessment of academic achievement would seem fundamental to an educational environment. Evaluating a child's academic progress can be of great value. Knowing what a child has assimilated, what skills have been mastered, and what individual strengths and weaknesses a child has can be of tremendous use in maximizing a child's academic progress. However, interpreting academic achievement in terms of grade equivalents, although superficially forthright, may inaccurately depict a child's academic achievement.

Grade equivalents are understandably well liked in reporting a child's school progress. A child is in the third grade, and the teacher, administration, and parents would like to know if this child is achieving at the third grade level. One could define specific information and skills imparted and then assess what had or had not been learned. However, rather than discussing content, teaching, and specific skills learned, an easier method for reporting academic achievement is to provide a solitary index: Lefty has a grade equivalent of 1.9 in Language Punctuation. Although one might not know what was taught or what was learned, if Lefty were in the first grade, a grade equivalent of 1.9 seems—well, a grade equivalent of 1.9 in the first grade makes sense.

Grade equivalents are offered with most achievement tests as a method for reporting raw scores and are frequently sought after by parents, teachers, administrators, and researchers. Paradoxically, grade equivalents have been the recipient of much derision and disavowal. Cronbach (1970) stated that "this is as good a place as any to mention—and condemn—a popular but archaic conversion known as 'age equivalents' and 'grade equivalents'" (p. 98).* Psychometricians are not at all reluctant to recite the evils of grade equivalents, and test manuals openly explain the pitfalls of these much-used indices. The manual for the Metropolitan Achievement Test (Primary I Battery) (Durost, 1959) stated that "experience has shown, too, that grade equivalents are subject to certain types of misinterpretation

---

* Grade equivalents indicate the median grade level associated with a raw score, and age equivalents signify the median age level associated with a raw score.

by parents and even by teachers with respect to appropriate pupil classification or grading" (p. 18).

Despite the awareness that grade equivalents have numerous limitations and can actually distort or misrepresent a child's academic achievement, they are still offered in achievement test manuals and used extensively to describe a child's academic progress. The reason why this is so is well known by those who provide grade equivalents to report a child's progress. Grade equivalents are used because "they're easy to understand." They might be misleading and a poor reflection of a child's performance in school, but they appear to be so simple, so descriptive of a child's progress that they remain a major score for describing a child's achievement status.

Criticisms of grade equivalents can be broken down into conceptual deficiencies and technical deficiencies. The conceptual deficiencies will be presented first, and after reviewing the method used to determine grade equivalents, the technical deficiencies will be discussed.

There is no reason to assume that an achievement test does not measure what was achieved in a school setting. However, the majority of achievement tests used in the United States were developed to be used on a national scale. The premise is that all children in all schools in all parts of the country are presented with the same knowledge, information, and skills which are measured by one of these "national" achievement tests. Such tests fail to take into account the great possibility that content will vary, material presented will vary, and that the method for imparting information and skills will vary. On a similar basis, the majority of achievement tests used provide national norms. If a child received a grade equivalent of 5.7, he is not achieving at the fifth grade and seventh month in the school he's attending, but he is achieving at the fifth grade and seventh month in comparison to a "national" grading scheme, which exists only in the mind of the test developer.

If an index is used, it should at least give some idea of a child's academic progress. Achievement tests are usually constructed with a limited number of items. This is necessary since a large number of test items would be impossible to administer, and the cost for constructing such a test would be prohibitive. However real these restraints are, many achievement tests use so few items on certain sections that the resulting grade equivalents are absolutely unacceptable. On one nationally known achievement test, a test of modest repute, a difference of one raw score point on one of the subtests at the upper age level will result in a grade equivalent difference of over two years!

A last general criticism of grade equivalents is that they do not indicate grade equivalence. If a first grade child received a grade equivalent of 3.5 on a word knowledge achievement test (associating pictures with printed words), this would not signify that this child knew all the printed words taught at the third grade level. A grade equivalent of 3.5 by a first grade child would only indicate that for that test the child correctly answered a number of items similar to the number of items answered correctly by many third graders. If only seven or eight correct answers separate a grade equivalent of 1.5 and 3.5, one could not unequivocally equate the quantitative and qualitative "word knowledge" of a first grade and third grade child.

GRADE EQUIVALENTS

The following example will help illustrate how grade equivalents are found and why they are so susceptible to technical deficiencies. A series of arithmetic problems was administered to a second, third, and fourth grade class. For each class, percentile ranks were determined. These results indicated that the median score for a second grade child was 7 correct, the median score for a third grade child was 14 correct, and the median score for a fourth grade child was 18 correct. As stated previously, the median, or a score with a percentile rank of 50, indicates that point at which 50 percent of the scores are above and 50 percent of the scores are below. As an example, if five children received scores of 0, 15, 8, 7, and 3, the median would be a raw score of 7; or, stated differently, a raw score of 7 would have a corresponding percentile rank of 50.

Assume further that the tests were administered in the fifth month of the school year (January). Figure 7 shows how grade equivalents were determined. Each median score was plotted against the grade level associated with that score. Since the median score for the second grade class was 7, a point was marked in Figure 7 corresponding to a raw score of 7 on the raw score axis and a grade level of 2.5 on the garde level axis. A grade level of 2.5 was used instead of a grade level of 2.0 because the children were tested in the fifth month of the second grade. This procedure was repeated for the third and fourth grade median scores. For the third grade a point was marked corresponding to a raw score of 14 and a grade level of 3.5; and for the fourth grade a point was marked corresponding to a raw score of 18 and a grade level of 4.5. The median grade level points in Figure 7 were then connected by a solid line.

Grade equivalents were determined by taking each raw score and finding the corresponding grade level. As an example, a raw score of 11 was equivalent to a grade level of 3.0. This is shown in Figure 7 by a dotted line extending from a raw score of 11 to the solid line, and then extending downward to a grade level of 3.0. Therefore, a child who received a raw score of 11

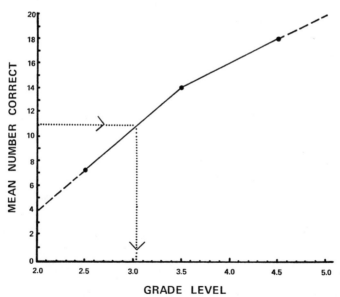

Figure 7.   An example showing how grade equivalents are found.

would be said to have a grade equivalent of 3.0. The dashed line below 2.5 and above 4.5 shows how grade equivalents are determined for very low and very high scores. By extending the solid line upward, one can estimate that a raw score of 20 corresponds to a grade equivalent of 5.0. Since fifth grade children were not given this test, a grade equivalent of 5.0 corresponding to a raw score of 20 is little more than an "educated" guess—and a guess in some instances that can be very misleading.

Table XIII presents the raw scores and grade equivalents determined from the information presented in Figure 7.

TABLE XIII

TABLE OF RAW SCORES AND CORRESPONDING GRADE EQUIVALENTS

Score	Grade Equivalent
4	2.0
5	2.2
6	2.3
7	2.5
8	2.6
9	2.8
10	2.9
11	3.0
12	3.2
13	3.3
14	3.5
15	3.7
16	4.0
17	4.3
18	4.5
19	4.7
20	5.0

SCALE LIMITATIONS

A scale is a set of numbers used to indicate a person's performance on a test. Just as a weight scale is used to indicate how heavy or light (depending on physical fitness) an individual is, a test scale is used to signify a person's test performance. Many of the major faults of grade equivalents involve scale limitations.

In the example just presented (see Table XIII) there are obvious grade equivalent scale inequalities. A raw score of 10 is equal to a grade equivalent of 2.9, a raw score of 15 is equal to a grade equivalent of 3.7, but a raw score of 20 is equal to a grade equivalent of 5.0. The grade equivalent difference between raw scores of 10 and 15 is 0.8, but the grade equivalent difference between raw scores of 15 and 20 is 1.3.

To show how great grade equivalent scale inequalities can be, consider the following example. A thirty item test measuring the primary multiplication facts (e.g., $5 \times 6 =$ ——, $7 \times 8 =$ ——) was administered to groups of second, third, fourth, and fifth grade children. The median scores were found to be 5 for the second grade children, 20 for the third grade children, 28 for the fourth grade children, and 29 for the fifth grade children. If the children were tested in the seventh month of the school year, 5 correct would be equal to a grade equivalent of 2.7, 20 correct would be equal to 3.7, 28 correct would be equal to 4.7, and 29 would be equal to 5.7. Fifteen raw score points separate the second and third grade children, but only one raw score point separates the fourth and fifth grade children.

From the foregoing discussion one can see how important median score values are in determining grade equivalents. Yet, there are many factors that can affect median score values and, as a result, play havoc with a grade equivalent scale. Median values might be too high or too low as a result of poor sampling, using a small sample, the uniqueness of the test items, or item difficulty. Whatever the cause, inaccurate or "unusual" median score values can seriously affect a grade equivalent scale. These problems become even more acute when grade equivalents are estimated. In Figure 7 a dashed line extended upward to estimate what grade level corresponded to a raw score of 20. This method for estimating grade equivalents revealed that a raw score of 20 was equal to a grade score of 5.0. However, a group of children exactly five years of age might not have had a median score value of 20. If the median score value of a group of children five years of age was approximately equal to the median score value of children tested in the fourth grade, then estimating that a raw score of 20 corresponded to a grade level of 5.0 would be inaccurate.

In addition to the many real and potential scale deficiencies of grade equivalents, these scores have also been criticized because grade equivalents achieved on different tests are not usually comparable. If a child received a grade equivalent of 2.5 on a language test, and a grade equivalent of 1.5 on a spelling test, and the mean for both tests was 3.0, we might assume that this child was half a year behind in language and a year and a half behind in spelling. However, if the standard deviation was 0.5 for the language test and 1.5 for the spelling test, this child would be one standard deviation below the mean in language [$(2.5 - 3.0) / 0.5 = -1.0$] and also one standard deviation below the mean in spelling [$(1.5 - 3.0 / 1.5 = -1.0$].

Comparing and interpreting grade equivalents is not only difficult but at times downright perplexing. On the Peabody Individual Achievement Test (Dunn and Markwardt, 1970), if a child seven years and ten months of age received a general information subtest raw score of 10, the percentile rank corresponding to this raw score is 7, and the grade equivalent corresponding to a raw score of 10 is 0.3. If this same child received a raw score of 15 on the spelling subtest, the percentile rank corresponding to this raw score is 4, and the grade equivalent corresponding to a raw score of 15 is 1.0. The problem is this: how do we compare general information and spelling (or even interpret general information and spelling) if the percentile rank in general information (7) is higher than the percentile rank in spelling (4), but the grade equivalent in spelling (1.0) is higher than the grade equivalent in general information (0.3)? One might ask why one would want to compare general information and spelling to begin with. That is another matter, but the fact is that interpreting and comparing these two subtests is not facilitated by the use of grade equivalent scores.

Grade equivalents are said to be used for several reasons including the following: (1) determining a child's strengths and weaknesses, (2) planning instruction, (3) grouping pupils, (4) maintaining a record of a child's academic progress, and (5) for the many grants, reports, and documents requiring information pertaining to a school or a district's academic status. Grade equivalents are used because of their apparent simplicity and because they are believed to be easily understood. However grade equivalents are used or whatever benefits grade equivalents might yield, these indices should be regarded as only a superficial reflection of a child's academic progress. If a child's progress in school is of concern, then what was taught should be assessed and what specifically was learned should be measured. When a decision is going to be made that concerns a child, we are being irresponsible if we fail to consider the child and what a child can and cannot do. If we use only grade equivalents, if we do not seek to understand what these indices mean (request a copy of the test and a test manual), we are demonstrating an unforgivable disregard for a child's worth.

Chapter Six

A QUESTIONABLE FRAME OF REFERENCE

STANDARDIZATION SAMPLES

W HEN A CHILD receives a percentile rank or standard score, a comparison is being made; a child's test score is being compared to a specific group. This group to which a child's test score is compared or referred has several labels including the following: norm group, normative group, reference group, and standardization sample. The group to which a child's test score is compared is the standard by which test performance is evaluated.

Unless the content of a test is known, a raw score is meaningless. There would be absolutely no worth in reporting that a child received a raw score of 14 on a vocabulary test without indicating the number and type of items given. A score on a test, in and of itself, has no intrinsic meaning. There are several methods for interpreting a child's test performance, and comparing a child's score to the scores of a specified group of children is undoubtedly the most widely used.

A child received a percentile rank of 56, and a statement is made that 56 percent of the children in the standardization sample had scored lower than this child scored. If the standardization sample was comprised of 200 second grade children, a statement might also be made that 56 percent of children "similar" to those who comprised the standardization sample had scored lower than this child scored. However, reporting that 56 percent of first grade children, 56 percent of third grade children, or 56 percent of all children had scored lower than this child scored would be incorrect. There is no such thing as "a child's IQ," or "a child's reading level." Standard scores, IQs, grade equivalents, and percentile ranks only have meaning because of the normative group on which they are based. Therefore, a child's performance on a test should be reported as "a percentile rank of 78 when compared to a national sample of 10-year-old children," or "a grade equivalent of 2.3 when compared to eighth grade children attending public schools in Odessa, Texas."

Prior to actually constructing a test, a test maker will have identified a population for whom the test was intended. This group for whom the test is appropriate is called a population. As an example, a population might be school age children living in the Midwest, or children between the ages of five and fifteen, or all first, second, and third grade children. In most instances the population specified will be quite large—all first, second, and third grade children would be a sizeable number. Because of time and cost factors, a test maker will most often draw a sample of children to estimate the test performance of children in the specified population. This, then, is the standardization sample.

Assume that a test was constructed to be used with all kindergarten children in the United States. Recoiling from the thought of testing all kindergarten children in the United States, the fearless test maker decided to use a sample of all kindergarten children in the United States. He decided to use a sample of 100 children. There is no rule as to how large a sample must be, but only that the sample fairly represent the specified population. A standardization sample might be as small as 50 (terribly small) or as many as 500,000 (frightfully large).

The test was administered to 100 kindergarten children attending schools in ten different states. The mean score for this sample of 100 children was found to be 24.0. Later, once norms had been developed, a score of 24 on this test would be interpreted as being equivalent to the mean performance of all kindergarten children in the United States. This interpretation would be fine—providing that the sample of 100 children was a fair representation of all kindergarten children. If by chance alone the test maker selected 100 "very bright" children, a mean of 24.0 would likely be much higher than the mean of the population of all kindergarten children. On the other hand, selecting an inordinate number of chidren who were still adjusting to the kindergarten experience might result in a mean score that was an underestimate of the population mean.

When a sample value (the mean test score in the above example) differs from a population value, sampling error is said to have occurred. To the dismay of educational testing, population values are more mystery than fact; population values are not generally known. As a result, common sense plays an important role in determining how representative a sample is. Very small samples or samples selected in such a way so as not to represent the intended population can affect the interpretation of a child's test performance.

Test developers expend considerable time, effort, and money selecting and testing normative samples. Enormous attention is paid to the selection of samples in order to ensure adequate sample size, but little thought is given to the meaningfulness of a test when constructed for a specified population. This is especially the case when the population is of a national order. If an achievement test is constructed for all fifth grade children in the United States, certain items will be appropriate for one school but inappropriate for another school. In other words, there is not one curriculum or one method for teaching skills and concepts that can be assessed by one test. For a test to be appropriate with a larger population, sensitivity to the uniqueness of each segment of that population is overlooked. A school in Jackson, Mississippi, may have a different curriculum, different textbook series, and different achievement expectations than a school in Flint, Michigan. Yet, children in both schools might be given the same achievement test. To be somewhat appropriate for each school, skills and concepts achieved that are unique to each school must be ignored in lieu of what both schools probably have in common.

Tests which purport to measure intelligence are no different than achievement tests in attempting to construct one instrument that is appropriate for a single population, which is composed of heterogeneous components and subcomponents. A set of vocabulary items is selected that is supposedly within the grasp of all—but what of urban, rural, and black vocabularies? Surely a test comprised of twenty or so items would not be sensitive to the varied experiences and backgrounds of all children in the United States.

Test makers are well aware of the limitations of national norms. After all, what exactly does a grade equivalent of 1.9 mean? There is no "national" first grade, there are thousands of different first grade classes. Saying that a child has a grade equivalent of 1.9 sounds meaningful until an attempt is made to conceptualize what a grade equivalent with a national frame of reference signifies. Furthermore, comparing a child to a national group tells nothing about how a child is performing in relation to those in his class, school, or district.

To compensate for the conceptual ambiguity of national norms, test makers often encourage test users to develop local norms. That is, a sample from a school or district is used as a frame of reference. In cases where a testing company provides a scoring service, scores derived from local norms are often provided along with scores derived from national norms. As meaningful and relevant as local norms might appear, national norms are often the sole reference group for comparing a child's test performance. This is the result of test makers not detailing how local norms can be developed (other than referring a user to one of the "many statistics books available"), apprehension on the part of test users regarding their ability to determine local norms (they are actually quite easy to develop), and a misguided belief that because a norm table provides corresponding percentile ranks, standard scores, or grade equivalents, the sample from which these scores were derived is really of minor importance. When a score might affect a child's life, nothing is really of minor importance.

REPRESENTATIVE CHILDREN

How are samples selected? Ideally, the selection of a sample should involve some type of randomized process. Random samples are looked on with high esteem in measurement and statistics. To illustrate how a random sample might be selected, consider the following example. A test maker defined a population of 800 children. Unable to test all 800 children, he decided to administer his test to a sample of 100. In order to select a random sample, he placed the name of each child who was in the population of 800 on a slip of paper, placed all the name slips in a large hat, blindly shuffled the slips about, and then with eyes closed drew 100 names. Barring horrible luck, the 100 children selected would likely provide a fair estimate of the test performance of the 800 children who comprised the entire population.

Random sampling has many virtues as well as several practical limitations. If a national sample were defined creating a situation where each child had an equal probability of being selected for inclusion in a sample, sampling would be an impossible task. Not even the most punctilious researcher would set about to record the names of all children in the United States at a specified age or grade level—not to mention the size of hat needed if the sample selected were so large.

In the development of a test the impracticalities of random sampling frequently give way to a type of quota sampling. For a national sample this might involve selecting a sample of children who represented salient characteristics of the population. Using United States census data, a researcher might select children in accordance with the national breakdown of males and females, whites and nonwhites, urban and rural children, and children drawn from various occupational groups (e.g., professional, skilled worker, farm worker). The representativeness of a sample would then be judged, for the most part, in terms of how close the characteristics of the sample approximated the characteristics of the defined population.

Sampling procedures will vary from one test to another. A group test might be administered to so many children that hugeness of sample size might be deemed more important than what children (or geographic regions) were sampled. Just as badly, many tests are normed by what can be described as "available" sampling techniques. Rather than traipsing about the countryside sampling at random or filling quotas, a test maker might use "available" children. If the test maker lived in Tuscaloosa, the standardization sample would be comprised of children living in Tuscaloosa. If a test maker lived in Twin Falls, the standardization sample would be comprised of children living in Twin Falls.

Somewhere between random, quota, and available sampling,

standardization samples are selected. Although selected and tested, the populations to which these samples refer are not always clearly defined. As an example, the Peabody Picture Vocabulary Test (Dunn, 1965) was standardized on "white children and youth residing in and around Nashville (Tennessee)" (p. 27). In all, 4,012 individuals were assessed. The author then stated that "certain precautions were taken so as to provide norms which should be useful throughout the United States" (p. 27). What precautions could be taken to make a test standardized in Nashville, Tennessee, appropriate for children living in Brooklyn, New York? If a test was standardized in Nashville, it would seem most appropriate for children living in Nashville. Likewise, a test standardized in Brooklyn, would seem most appropriate for children living in Brooklyn. Yet, the test manual for the Peabody Picture Vocabulary Test provides a suggestion that this test would be useful throughout the United States.

Test makers most often select children on the basis of age and/or grade level. As mentioned before, if quota sampling is used, socioeconomic level, geographic area, sex, or urban-rural residence might be considered when selecting children. Occasionally, however, a standardization sample is so out of the ordinary that a meaningful interpretation of a child's test performance, beyond those included in the sample, is impossible. The Northwestern Syntax Screening Test (Lee, 1971) was standardized on groups ranging in size from 34 to 160. In addition to several ridiculously low sample sizes, the author stated that the "children came from middle-income and upper middle-income communities and from homes where standard American dialect was spoken" (p. 5). Although not stated, an acknowledgements section in the test manual (Lee, 1971, p. 10) indicated that the "norms" were developed using children primarily in and about Evanston, Illinois. The thought that norms for this test, developed from the samples described, would be used with children throughout the United States is a sad commentary on tests and the interpretation of test scores.

Even the best intentioned test developer can encounter serious conceptual problems when attempting to select a "suitable" reference group. Let us imagine a test maker who desired to use a group of "average" children as a frame of reference for interpreting test scores. At a superficial level this makes sense since children are usually described as being above or below "average." The test maker then selected children who were doing average work in school, who had average IQ scores, who were average physically, and who came from average homes. After this tedious process of selecting average children was completed, the test was given and norms were determined. The completed norm table revealed that percentile ranks ranged from 1 to 99 (as is usually the case). But wait! How can this be? All children were average, and now the norms reveal that some "average" children have below average scores—insomuch as a percentile rank of 1 would probably be interpreted as being below average. And if a child from outside the standardization group was tested, a child who was also "average," using the "average" group as a frame of reference might suggest that this child was below average. As you can see, conceptualizing an "average" child as being below average when compared to "average" children is not a simple matter.

Norms will vary, samples and sampling techniques will vary; but if a test is given, and a child's performance is compared to the performance of a normative group, then the test user is obligated to examine and know the characteristics of that reference group.

CRITERION-REFERENCED TESTS

Normative testing, comparing a child's test score to a standardization group, is not the only method for evaluating performance. Instead of comparing a child's performance on a test to a norm group, test performance can be interpreted in terms of how well a child knows the content. This form of testing comes under the rubric of criterion-referenced testing. On a norm-referenced test (e.g., those tests that result in percentile ranks, standard scores, and grade equivalents), a child's score is referred to a norm group; on a criterion-referenced test a child's performance is referred to specific content and a criterion or acceptable performance is specified.

The following will show the difference between a norm- and

criterion-referenced interpretation of a child's test score. On the Stanford Diagnostic Arithmetic Test (Beatty, Madden, and Gardner, 1966) Level II, a perfect score (20) on the addition and subtraction subtest by a child above the second half of the seventh grade will result in a percentile rank of 70. Stating that 30 percent of the children in a standardization group scored above a child who received a perfect score is meaningless. A more sensible presentation of a perfect score in this situation would be to simply state that 20 addition and subtraction facts were answered correctly. In addition, a description or examples of the types of items tested could also be given. A norm-referenced test compares, a criterion-referenced test indicates type of behavior or performance.

Many individuals involved with educational testing equate the quality of a test with how well it discriminates. However, discriminating among children (e.g., low, average, and high) might be scintillating psychometrically, but it is not always beneficial for a specific child's educational progress. A teacher administered a readiness test (e.g., "Make a mark on the letter k."). One child identified 5 letters and received a score of 5, while a second child identified six letters and received a score of 6. The "norms" indicated that scores between 6 and 10 were within the "average" range, and that scores between 3 and 5 were "below average." One point might discriminate these two children, but to say that knowing one more letter warrants dichotomizing children into "average" and "below average" groups is ludicrous.

Explaining a child's performance on a test in terms of content is practical enough but not without potential faults. All too often, emphasis on test content results in learning trivia or, even worse, learning the answers to a single test. As an example, one researcher set out to demonstrate that a course with specific objectives was far more effective than a course without objectives. In one class the material was assigned, discussed the following day, and a test was given. In a second class objectives were first given, the material then assigned and discussed the following day, and a test given. The objectives went something like "Be able to indicate, using a multiple choice format, in what year Columbus discovered America." As expected, the experimental class, the class that received the objectives, knew more answers than the control class, the class that did not receive objectives. This study proved two things. First, children will perform better on tests if they are first given the answers. Second, the difference between research and scholarship can be vast.

A tendency toward factual information and difficulty in designating acceptable performance levels (How much content should a child know before a new content area is presented?) are definite limitations of criterion-referenced testing. In addition, criterion-referenced testing is not especially amendable to the plethora of statistics thought to be so vital when discussing norm-referenced tests. Regardless of these deficiencies, there seems little harm in attempting to translate a child's performance or score on a test into a meaningful description of the type of work a child can or cannot do. A parent is entitled to more than a statistical explanation of standard scores, percentile ranks, or grade equivalents when asking what a score on a test means. What a child knows is just as important as how well a child performs when compared to others. Criterion-referenced testing may not be the salvation of educational testing, but it certainly is an alternative to norm-referenced testing.

Chapter Seven

PROOF BY NUMBER

RELATIONSHIPS

CORRELATIONS ARE USED to show relationships. If two tests were given to a group of children, and children who received high scores on the first test also received high scores on the second test, and children who received low scores on the first test also received low scores on the second test, the scores of these two tests are related. High scores on the first test are related (i.e., correlated) with high scores on the second test, and low scores on the first test are related with low scores on the second test. In this example the relationship is said to be positive; that is, there is a positive correlation between scores on the first test and scores on the second test. A positive correlation indicates that as scores move from below average to above average on one test, there will be a similar (positive) increase in corresponding scores on a second test.

An example of a positive correlation between two sets of scores is shown in Table XIV. The first set of scores is intended to represent scores on a kindergarten reading readiness test, and the second set of scores is intended to signify first grade scores on a reading vocabulary test. As an example, Jane received a readiness score of 18 in kindergarten. One year later Jane was tested again by means of a reading vocabulary test, and her grade equivalent was found to be 2.4. Unlike Jane, Gunther received a relatively low readiness score of 4. His grade equivalent one year later was found to be 0.6.

The correlation between readiness scores and reading vocabulary grade equivalents shown in Table XIV is positive. This means that a high score on reading readiness will likely result in a high score on reading vocabulary and that a low score on

TABLE XIV

EXAMPLE OF KINDERGARTEN READING READINESS SCORES
AND FIRST GRADE READING VOCABULARY SCORES

Child	Readiness Scores	Vocabulary Scores
Jane	18	2.4
Louie	4	1.1
Lefty	3	1.5
Fred	12	1.4
Mary	14	1.6
Homer	7	1.0
Gunther	4	0.6
Herman	10	1.2
Tulip	16	1.2
Nancy	9	1.4

reading readiness will likely result in a low score on reading vocabulary. Note, however, that although the general relationship between reading readiness and reading vocabulary is positive, there are exceptions. Tulip received a 16 on reading readiness and a grade equivalent of 1.2, while Herman received a reading readiness score of 10 but a grade equivalent in reading vocabulary identical to that of Tulip's. A correlation indicates a relationship (or lack of a relationship) between two tests. However, a correlation is not a rule, and a score on one test does not mandate a related score on a second test. Just as a child's behavior will vary, so will a child's test scores.

To further illustrate the concept of correlation, the reading readiness and reading vocabulary scores shown in Table XIV are graphically presented in Figure 8. Each pair of scores was graphed by first finding the readiness score on the horizontal axis and then moving upward until the corresponding grade equivalent was found. For Lefty, a point was plotted corresponding to a score of 3 on the reading readiness axis and a grade equivalent of 1.5 on the reading vocabulary axis. As shown, there is a general tendency for low reading readiness scores to correspond to low reading vocabulary scores and for high reading readiness scores to correspond to high reading vocabulary scores. Again, remember that the general relationship between reading readiness and reading vocabulary scores is positive and not that a reading readiness score dictates what a reading vocabulary score will be.

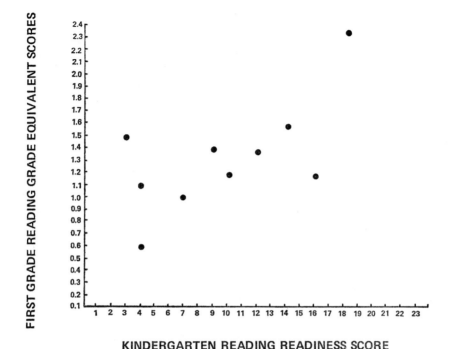

Figure 8. A graph (or scatter plot) showing the relationship between reading readiness and reading vocabulary scores.

Correlations give credibility to scores, believability to test norms, and confidence to test users. Correlations are used to predict, prove, and relate.* Correlations give vitality, if not life,

---

* There are several methods available for determining the validity of a test (what a test measures) including: face validity (what a test appears to measure), content validity (evaluation of test content by experts), discriminant validity (showing that correlations between a test and dissimilar tests are low), convergent validity (showing that correlations between a test and similar tests are high), and predictive validity (how well a test predicts what it purports to predict). In the world of educational testing, face validity is held in low esteem, content validity demands understanding and common sense, while the last three types of validity mentioned are usually determined by correlational techniques. For the most part, when validity coefficients (correlations) are reported for a test they are not used, are ignored, or are interpreted in such a way so as to confuse basic issues. Nonetheless, they are statistically pleasing and therefore tremendously popular. The task of the test user is not so much actually using validity coefficients but rather trying to remember the various names used to establish a test's validity (e.g., content, criterion, construct, face, discriminant, convergent, concurrent, item, factorial, congruent).

to educational testing. Most test manuals reek of correlations, and many tests are evaluated more on the variety of correlations they have to offer rather than actual usefulness.

The study of correlations would be simple if all relationships were perfect and positive. Not only are relationships usually less than perfect, but the relationship between two tests can be something other than positive. Table XV shows scores for five children on four measures. The relationship between math scores and teacher ratings of school work (ranging from a poor rating of 0 to an excellent rating of 10) is positive. In this example the relationship is also perfect. In the real world such perfection is unlikely. This example is intended to illustrate a type of relationship and not to suggest the unlikely occurrence of a perfect relationship.

TABLE XV

SCORES ILLUSTRATING POSITIVE, NEGATIVE, AND
CURVILINEAR CORRELATIONS

Child	Math	School Work	Attention	Draw-a-Bat Test
Louie	5	4	8	7
Lefty	10	6	6	2
Herman	15	8	4	9
Tulip	0	2	10	5
Mary	20	10	2	1

Exactly opposite the relationship between math and school work scores, the relationship between math and teacher ratings of attention is negative. Tulip received the lowest math score but the highest teacher rating of attention. Conversely, Mary received the highest math score but the lowest teaching rating of attention.

If positive and negative correlations were not enough, the relationship between math scores and scores on a perceptual-motor device called the draw-a-bat test is curvilinear.* In other

---

* The majority of correlation problems involve finding the best direct (or indirect) relationship between two variables. Such relationships are referred to as being linear (e.g., a high score on test A is associated with a high score on test B, and a low score on test A is associated with a low score on test B). If a relationship does not follow a linear rule (e.g., part of the relationship is positive, and part of the relationship is negative), the relationship is said to be curvilinear.

words, the relationship between high draw-a-bat scores and math scores is positive, but the relationship between low draw-a-bat scores and math is negative. A curvilinear relationship can best be explained by means of a graphic representation. The solid line in Figure 9 signifies the positive relationship between math scores and school work ratings. The dashed line represents the negative relationship between math scores and attention ratings. The dotted line denotes the curvilinear relationship between math scores and draw-a-bat scores.

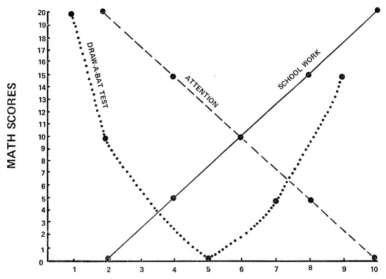

Figure 9. An example of positive, negative, and curvilinear relationships. The horizontal axis indicates scores on the draw-a-bat test (which is not copyrighted), the attention scale, and the school work scale.

The existence of a relationship is more important than whether a relationship is negative or positive. The fact that a relationship is positive does not mean that it is the least bit "better" than a negative relationship. A negative relationship is just as meaningful (and meaningful does not imply useful) as a positive relationship. Likewise, a curvilinear relationship can be just as meaningful as either a positive or negative relationship.

CORRELATION COEFFICIENTS

A correlation will vary between +1.0 and −1.0. A correlation of +1.0 is a perfect positive correlation, and a correlation of −1.0 is a perfect negative correlation. A correlation of 0.0 indicates no relationship between two tests. In research reports, correlations will be reported as being between +1.0 and −1.0 (e.g., "The correlation between IQ scores and reading was found to be .673.").

The correlation between two tests can be found using z scores. An example is presented in Table XVI showing the test scores of five children tested on two different occasions. The mean of the first test is 2.0 and the standard deviation is .894. The mean is subtracted from each raw score and these values are divided by the standard deviation in order to determine z scores. On the first test, a raw score of 2 results in a z score of 0.000 [(2 − 2.0) / .894 = 0.000], a raw score of 3 results in a z score of +1.118 [(3 − 2.0) / .894 = +1.118], and a raw score of 1 results in a z score of −1.118 [(1 − 2.0) / .894 = −1.118].

The mean of the second test is 4.0 and the standard deviation is 1.897. On this test, a raw score of 4 results in a z score of 0.000 [(4 − 4.0) / 1.897 = 0.000], a raw score of 7 results in a z score of +1.581 [(7 − 4.0) / 1.897 = +1.581], a raw score of 5

TABLE XVI

CALCULATION OF CORRELATION USING z SCORES

Child	First Test Raw Score	z Score	Second Test Raw Score	z Score	Multiply First Test and Second Test z Scores
Homer	2	0.000	4	0.000	0.000
Gunther	3	+1.118	7	+1.581	+1.768
Jane	3	+1.118	5	+0.527	+0.589
Nancy	1	−1.118	2	−1.054	+1.178
Lefty	1	−1.118	2	−1.054	+1.178
					Sum = +4.713

$\Sigma z_X z_Y$ (Sum of z score products) $= +4.713$

Correlation (r)

$$r = \frac{\Sigma z_X z_Y}{N}$$

$$r = \frac{+4.713}{5}$$

$$r = 0.943$$

results in a z score of +0.527 [(5 − 4.0) / 1.897 = +0.527], and a raw score of 2 results in a z score of −1.054 [(2 − 4.0) / 1.897 = −1.054].

The z scores indicate each child's performance relative to the mean score of each test. Homer scored at the mean on each test and therefore received z scores of 0.000 on each test. Jane scored above the mean on the first test (z = +1.118) and above the mean on the second test (z = +0.527). Lefty scored below the mean on the first test (z = −1.118) and below the mean on the second test (z = −1.054).

Once z scores have been determined, z scores on the first test are multiplied by z scores on the second test. This is stated symbolically as $z_X z_Y$, which shows that each child's z score on the first test (z_X) should be multiplied by his/her corresponding z score on the second test (z_Y). The product of Homer's z scores was found to be 0.000 (0.000 × 0.000 = 0.000); the product of Jane's z scores was found to be +0.589 (+1.118 × +0.527 = +0.589); and the product of Nancy's z scores was found to be +1.178 (−1.118 × −1.054 = +1.178). The z score products for each child's z scores are presented in the last column of Table XVI.

Following the calculation of z score products, the sum of these products is then found. In the present example the sum of z score products is +4.713. The correlation coefficient is then found by dividing the sum of z score products by the number of children, or stated as a formula:

$$r = \frac{\Sigma z_X z_Y}{N} \, ,$$

where r is the symbol used to indicate a correlation coefficient. For this example the correlation coefficient is found to be 0.943 (+4.713 / 5 = 0.943). In a report this might be stated as, "The correlation between first and second test scores was 0.943," or, "There was a high positive correlation (r = 0.943) between first and second test scores." Note that this is an example and that a correlation based on so few children would not likely be reported because of the possibility of a high correlation occurring by chance. The fewer the scores (or the smaller the N), the greater the possibility that chance can effect a correlation coefficient.

In the extreme case, a correlation found for two children would have to be high positive, high negative, or zero.

The calculation of a correlation coefficient using z scores demonstrates that a correlation indicates how z scores covary. If high z scores on one test correspond to high z scores on a second test, and low z scores on the first test correspond to low z scores on the second test, the resulting correlation will be positive. This means that there is a direct relationship between corresponding z scores.

Although conceptually useful in showing what a correlation is, the calculation of correlation coefficients using z scores can be a tedious task computationally—particularly when there are a great number of pairs of scores. Table XVII shows a method for calculating a correlation coefficient that is computationally efficient, although not as conceptually clear as the z score method. To find a correlation, means and standard deviations are first found. As already noted when finding z scores, the mean of the first test is 2.0 and the standard deviation is 0.894, while the mean of the second test is 4.0 and the standard deviation is 1.897. Using this information, the correlation coefficient can be found by the following formula:

$$ r = \frac{\dfrac{\Sigma XY}{N} - \overline{XY}}{SD_x SD_y} $$

TABLE XVII

CALCULATION OF CORRELATION USING RAW SCORES

Child	First Test X	X²	Second Test Y	Y²	Multiple First Test and Second Test Raw Scores
Homer	2	4	4	16	2 × 4 = 8
Gunther	3	9	7	49	3 × 7 = 21
Jane	3	9	5	25	3 × 5 = 15
Nancy	1	1	2	4	1 × 2 = 2
Lefty	1	1	2	4	1 × 2 = 2
Sums =	10	24	20	98	48

$\overline{X} = 2$ $\overline{Y} = 4$ XY (Sum of gross products) = 48

$SD_x = 0.894$ $SD_y = 1.897$

$$ r = \frac{\dfrac{\Sigma XY}{N} - \overline{XY}}{SD_x SD_y}, \quad \text{and} \quad \frac{\dfrac{48}{5} - (2)(4)}{(0.894)(1.897)}, \quad \text{so} \quad r = 0.943 $$

The symbol ΣXY is the sum of the raw score products and is found by multiplying each child's raw score on the first test by the corresponding score on the second test and then finding the sum of these products. The raw score products are presented in the last column of Table XVII, and the sum of these products is 48. Using the above formula, the correlation coefficient is found to be .943—a coefficient the same as that found using the z score method.

PREDICTING TEST SCORES

Finding a correlation can result in a feeling of security. An elegant formula, numerous computations, and an exact-sounding coefficient ("The correlation is .7016.") can falsely contribute to the meaningfulness or usefulness of a correlation. In educational testing, correlations have two primary uses: (1) to predict a child's performance or to suggest that a test has predictive capability, and (2) to show that two tests (or two sets of scores) are somehow related.

The *potential* use to predict a child's future performance is one of the most important features of a correlation coefficient. If the correlation between two tests were perfect, we could accurately state ("predict") that a z score on one test would have an identical corresponding z score on a second test. If we knew the correlation between two tests and we knew a child's z score on one test, we could predict this child's performance on a second test by the following formula:

$$\text{PREDICTED } z_Y = (r_{XY})\ (z_X)$$

This formula specifies that a z score on one test (test Y) can be predicted by multiplying the correlation between the two tests (r_{XY}) by the z score on a second test (test X). If a child's z score on one test is +2.00, and the correlation between this test and a second test is 0.70, then this child's predicted z score would be +1.40 ($0.70 \times +2.00 = +1.40$). If a child's z score on one test is +1.48, and the correlation between this test and a second test was 0.0, then this child's predicted z score would be 0.00. Stated differently, if the correlation between two tests is 0.0, the best prediction possible is to say that a child will score at the mean.

Just as z scores are primarily used to explain correlations rather than actually calculating correlations, predicting z scores is a little-used practice in educational testing. If a prediction is going to be made, a test user will want a more meaningful score than a bland, predicted z score. To achieve this, test users can use scores on one test to predict a score (e.g., raw score, grade equivalent) on a second test. The following example will illustrate how this is accomplished. In Table XIV two sets of scores were given: raw scores on a reading readiness test given in kindergarten and reading vocabulary grade equivalents determined in the first grade. Let us say that an administrator wished to use this information so that he could predict first grade reading vocabulary grade equivalents based on kindergarten reading readiness scores. He did this with the intent of offering special help for children with low predicted grade equivalents. In essence, he wanted to group the children. To predict grade equivalents he calculated the means and standard deviations for reading readiness scores and for reading vocabulary grade equivalents as well as determining the correlation between these two sets of scores. He found the mean reading readiness score to be 9.700 and the standard deviation to be 5.001. For the reading vocabulary grade equivalents he found the mean to be 1.340 and the standard deviation to be 0.445. He then used the following formula to predict first grade reading vocabulary grade equivalents where the correlation (0.652) is signified by r.

$$\text{PREDICTED} \quad Y = \bar{Y} + r\frac{SD_y}{SD_x}(X - \bar{X})$$

PREDICTED Y represents the predicted first grade reading vocabulary grade equivalents. If the reader has a disposition for formulas and predicting scores, the information supplied can be used to verify the accuracy of the predictions presented in Table XVIII. In this table, kindergarten reading readiness scores, predicted first grade reading vocabulary grade equivalents, and actual first grade reading vocabulary grade equivalents are shown.

TABLE XVIII

EXAMPLE OF READING VOCABULARY SCORES PREDICTED
FROM KINDERGARTEN READING READINESS SCORES

Child	Readiness Scores	Predicted Vocabulary Scores	Actual Vocabulary Scores
Jane	18	1.82	2.4
Louie	4	1.01	1.1
Lefty	3	0.95	1.5
Fred	12	1.47	1.4
Mary	14	1.59	1.6
Homer	7	1.18	1.0
Gunther	4	1.01	0.6
Herman	10	1.36	1.2
Tulip	16	1.71	1.2
Nancy	9	1.30	1.4

At this point you might be impressed with the oracular method for predicting scores, but wondering why an administrator would want to predict first grade reading vocabulary grade equivalents when he already had these scores. If this were a real example, predicting scores for children from whom the correlation between reading readiness and reading vocabulary was estimated serves only to indicate the degree to which predicted and actual scores differ. If predicted scores were actually to be used, scores would be predicted for children who had taken the readiness test but who had not taken the reading vocabulary test.

After suffering through the computational rigor of predicting z scores, don't be disheartened to learn that predicting a child's performance on some future test is fraught with risk. This is so for several reasons. In the first place, predicting a child's score on a second test after a period of time can be risky in that a child's performance will vary from age level to age level, from situation to situation, and from test to test. In Table XVIII Lefty had a readiness score of 3, a predicted score of 0.95, but an actual reading vocabulary grade equivalent of 1.5. A predicted score suggests accuracy, but there is no law, no universal rule that states that a child cannot excel beyond our wildest expectation. Within each child there is a potential that can never be measured. The difference between Lefty's predicted score and his actual score was small but still demonstrates that errors of prediction are more the rule than the exception. What is dangerous is that predicting a child's academic performance can so affect teaching and curriculum that achieving beyond the prediction is almost impossible. If a child's reading readiness score was found to be 3, and assignment to a low group was based on the predicted reading vocabulary grade equivalent of 0.95, who can say that given the same opportunities as other children, given one year to develop, this chlid would not have a grade equivalent of 1.5, or 2.5, or 3.5?

Correlations are more often used to suggest that a test has predictive capability than to actually predict a child's future test performance. A significant correlation is found between readiness and reading scores, which implies that children with low readiness scores "will" have low reading scores. A significant correlation is found between IQ scores and school grades, which implies that a child with a low IQ score "will" have low school grades. What is truly amazing is that some children have the capacity to rise above their predicted performance, even after teachers, administrators, and parents have been brainwashed as to what a child "will" and "will not" do.

When a correlation is reported there is usually reference made as to whether the correlation is significant. Prediction implies usefulness, while statistical significance suggests a finding of great importance. "The correlation between reading readiness and reading vocabulary is significant at the .05 level." This statement alludes to a very important finding and intimidates the reader not to dare question a correlation that is statistically significant.

Whether a correlation is statistically significant depends on two factors: the size of the sample from which the correlation is based and the size of the correlation. A small experiment will best convey the concept of statistical significance. Numbers 0 through 9 are placed on 10 separate slips of paper. Each slip is then folded and placed in a hat. The numbers are tossed about and, with eyes closed, a number is selected. This number is recorded, placed back in the hat and a second number selected. This procedure is repeated until five pairs of numbers have been selected: 8 and 1, 5 and 3, 4 and 8, 2 and 9, 7 and 5. The correlation for these pairs of random numbers is found to be −0.85. Although high, a negative correlation of this magnitude may have been the result of chance. If the first pair drawn had been 8 and 8 (instead of 8 and 1) and the third pair drawn had been 4 and 1 (instead of 4 and 8), the correlation would have been +0.03. With so few pairs an extremely high correlation is needed before statistical significance can be inferred.

Statistical significance is a state of satisfaction; an individual is satisfied that a correlation based on so many pairs did not occur by chance. In the above example, where the number of pairs is five, a correlation between −0.88 and +0.88 will occur by chance 95 percent of the time. This means that if we repeated the above experiment 100 times and calculated 100 different correlations, approximately 95 percent of the correlations would be between −0.88 and +0.88, and 5 percent of the correlations would be equal or greater than either −0.88 or +0.88. If a correlation is not based on random numbers, and five pairs were used, an individual might interpret a correlation equal to or greater than −0.88 as being statistically significant. A statement might be made that the correlation between test X and test Y, where $N=5$, is significant at the .05 level. This means that a correlation this large, based on five pairs, would occur by chance five times out of 100 if random numbers were used. If an individual were conservative, significance might not be claimed unless the possibility of a correlation occurring by chance was one in 100 or less. If an individual were to be extremely conservative, he might want the chance occurrence to be less than one in 1,000. Statistical tables are readily available (Guilford, 1956; Runyon and Haber, 1967) that indicate, based on the number of pairs, the chance occurrence (5 times out of 100, 1 out of 100) of correlation coefficients.

Statistical significance can easily conceal the real meaning underlying what a test measures. If a test purports to measure intelligence, to be valid it should measure intelligence. If a test claims to measure achievement, to be valid it should measure achievement. All too often the validity of a test (measuring what it says it measures) is a product of "significant" correlations and a peculiar brand of circular reasoning. The X intelligence test is being marketed—but who is to say whether this test is valid or not. A child cannot be opened up, his intelligence examined, and put back together. Not being able to do this, the X intelligence test is correlated with the Y intelligence test and the correlation is found to be significant. But is the Y intelligence test valid? To answer this question the Y intelligence test is correlated with the Z intelligence test and the correlation is found to be significant. Correlating one test with another to determine validity can go on ad infinitum, but we can terminate the process by proudly declaring that the correlation between the Z intelligence test and the X intelligence test is statistically significant. By doing this we create a tight circle, cemented by "statistical significance," which unabashedly testifies to test validity.

Statistical significance means only that a correlation is different from 0.0. If there are a great many pairs, a very small correlation will be "statistically significant." If there are 1000 pairs, a correlation as small as $+0.062$ will be said to be significant at the .05 level. This means that a correlation equal to or greater than -0.062 or $+0.062$ will occur by chance approximately five times out of 100. Needless to say, a correlation of $+0.062$ is low and for all practical purposes meaningless—but it does differ from 0.0 (at the .05 level), and "statistical significance" can be claimed.

A correlation may be a helpful guide for understanding what a test measures, but a significant correlation should not be used as an imprimatur for the goodness or usefulness of a test. The meaning of a test goes beyond a matrix of correlations; a child is something more than a predicted score.

Chapter Eight

SAY WHAT YOU MEAN,
NOT MEAN WHAT YOU SAY

TEST NAMES

COULD IT BE THAT the key to unraveling the mystery of educational testing is in understanding test names? Not that a test name has anything to do with what a test measures. On the contrary, a test name may only reflect a test maker's well-developed imagination. Still, much can be learned from a test name—a test maker's expectations, the perceived integrity, good will, validity, and importance of a test, or the group for whom a test was designed. A test name is not a trifling matter.

Intelligence test names are a case in point. Intelligence has been variously defined to include, or exclude, abstract intelligence, adaptive behavior, acquired information, verbal ability, social behavior, genetic material, problem solving, learning, and creativity. Yet, intelligence tests are not labeled "Intelligence Test of Social Ability," "Intelligence Scale of Acquired Information," or "Intelligence Measure of Creativity." An intelligence test is an intelligence test, even though one might emphasize stringing beads while another is comprised of a series of multiple-guess questions. The possibility that a test might measure a small or unique facet of a child's intellect would not inhibit a test maker from calling a test a TEST OF INTELLIGENCE. If this seems indefensible, the ultimate definition of intelligence could always be conjured up: a child's intelligence is what an intelligence test measures. Intelligence is not a product of nature, intelligence is created. And who can criticize that which creates?

This tendency for overstatement is not confined to tests that claim to measure intelligence. An achievement test designed for a national population might not be completely suitable for a given school or area. But surely such a test cannot be expected to be named The————Test of Many Areas Which Are Probably Achieved in School. Long tests and short tests, good tests and bad tests, appropriate tests and inappropriate tests—all are "achievement tests."

Once the major emphasis of a test has been decided (e.g., intelligence, achievement, reading), a dilemma arises concerning the establishment of a test's identity. Obviously, a test could not be called just A Test of Intelligence or, if the test maker were overly arrogant, *The* Test of Intelligence. A solution to this problem is to name a test in honor (if that is the correct term) of a university. This not only gives a test identity but associates a test with the prestige and scholarly image of a university. Although this is a common practice, giving examples is confounded by the fact that it is difficult to differentiate whether a test has been named after a university or a state—as in State of Illinois. The Peabody Picture Vocabulary Test (Dunn, 1965) was apparently named after George Peabody College for Teachers, but was the California Achievement Test (Tiegs and Clark, 1970) named after the State of California or the University of California? This should not suggest that a test named after a state is without prestige. As a matter of fact, what is amazing is that a test titled the United States Test of Intelligence or the United States Test of Achievement has not been marketed.

Determining whether a test was named after a state or a university can sometimes be resolved by noting the test author's university affiliation. If a test were called the Maine Test of General Knowledge (which could easily be misconstrued as the most important test of this class) and the test author were on the faculty at the University of Maine, a reasonable assumption would be that the test was named after the University of Maine. In any case, this confusion could be overcome if test makers used college or university nicknames to identify tests. The Razorback Test of Intelligence, the Buckeye Reading Scale, or the Wolverine Readiness Test are examples of test names which clearly signify (if you follow sports) the university to be honored, while at the same time providing a colorful label that honestly captures the competitiveness of educational tests.

If a test maker is not inclined to name a test after a state or university, using one's surname can produce melifluous titles. Examples of this are the Wechsler Intelligence Scale for Children (Wechsler, 1949) and the Lorge-Thorndike Intelligence Tests (Lorge and Thorndike, 1957). Finally, a test maker can always combine a university with a surname. The Stanford-Binet Intelligence Scale (Terman and Merrill, 1973) was named after Stanford University (which is in Stanford, California) and Alfred Binet, the French psychologist who first introduced the test. As a matter of record, using one's own name in labeling a test would seem the preferred method for identifying a test—authorship is specified and responsibility is assumed. At least if a test is bad or is ever demonstrated to be a psychometric abomination, it will be associated with the person who created the measure. Then again, this might be one reason to name a test after a university (or state).

A successful name has *élan,* a dimension of sophistication, and importance. The Illinois Test of Psycholinguistic Abilities (Kirk, McCarthy and Kirk, 1968) is one of the better sounding test names. Some reviewers feel that the name of this test is too ambitious. John Carroll (1972), in a brief article in Buros' *Seventh Mental Measurements Yearbook,* had this to say of the Illinois Test of Psycholinguistic Abilities (ITPA): "The title of the ITPA is a misnomer, and users should be cautioned to look carefully at the true nature of the test, which might less misleadingly have been named something like the 'Illinois Diagnostic Test of Cognitive Functioning'" (p. 819). The suggested name is not much of an improvement, but the problem is evident.

Because one reviewer was disturbed by an overzealous test title does not mean that every reviewer shares that concern. Following the Carroll article, Clinton Chase (1972) stated that "the revised ITPA allows the examiner to assess psycholinguistic behavior in more detail than the earlier edition, and does it with moderate reliability and with a fairly stable profile of scores" (p. 824). This is an example of an individual who is preoccupied with correlations and believes in the relationship between a test name and reality.

There are many decisions to be made when naming a test, and one of these is when to call a test a test. For example, the

Stanford-Binet Intelligence Scale is most certainly a test, but it is called a scale. The Wechsler Intelligence Scale for Children is another test referred to as a scale. The question then arises, does calling a test a scale make the scale a better test? Kerlinger (1973) provided an enlightening and entertaining explanation of tests and scales. He stated that "tests are scales, but scales are not necessarily tests. This can be said because scales do not ordinarily have the meanings of competition and success or failure that tests do. Significantly, we say 'achievement testing,' not 'achievement scaling'; 'intelligence testing' and not 'intelligence scaling'" (p. 492). If this is true, the Stanford-Binet Intelligence Scale and the Wechsler Intelligence Scale for Children are actually tests called scales that are used for intelligence testing.

Calling a test a scale is not a bad idea in that a scale does allude to accuracy. You stand on a scale and an indicator points to a weight. If you are underweight or overweight you might disagree with a scale, but everyone knows that scales are fairly accurate. Who can argue with fact—a number, arrived at by means of an objective instrument, that coldly states your true weight. An intelligence test called a scale suggests an instrument (educational testing is forever assuming scientific airs) that produces a score that is dispassionate and scientifically accurate.

Referring to a test as a scale is not the only option allowed a test maker. A test can always be called a survey, which allows a test to be used as a test but not burdened by the negative connotation which the word *test* brings. A survey hints that an area (e.g., reading, readiness) is going to be inspected and studied. Roach and Kephart (1966) stated that the Purdue Perceptual-Motor Survey (believed to be named after the university in Indiana) "is *not* a test. It is a survey which allows the practitioner to observe a broad spectrum of behavior within a structured, but not stereotyped, set of circumstances" (p. iii). They also stated that their survey "is written for the practitioner" and "to provide the teacher with a tool which can be used to identify those children who do not possess perceptual-motor abilities necessary for acquiring academic skills by the usual instructional methods" (p. iii). Not only does "survey" misleadingly connote a comprehensive analysis (or at least a valid analysis), but deciding who does and who does not possess "perceptual-motor abilities" seems to be a very testlike decision.

The sensitivity of a test to evaluate a child's skill or level of knowledge in a given area can also be incorporated in a test name. If a test was constructed to diagnose a problem or problems, but common sense indicates that because of shoddy construction, the superficiality of the test, or one of many psychometric problems the test is not valid, the test can innocently be referred to as a screening instrument or screening test. A screening test intimates the possibility of a problem but defers complete responsibility by announcing that "additional" testing is necessary.

On the test sensitivity continuum, diagnostic tests are opposite screening tests. A diagnostic test should help to formulate hypotheses as to why a child does not perform, and not simply how he performs when compared to others. A reading diagnostic test might assess oral reading, silent reading, syllabication (e.g., breaking a word down into syllables), sound blending (i.e., putting together sounds to form words), and auditory discrimination. Diagnostic tests can be useful providing three criteria are met: the areas assessed are meaningful, the method used to assess these areas provides useful information, and enough information is assessed in each area to better understand a child's behavior. "Diagnosing" a child's reading without considering oral reading could seem a neglectful method for understanding a child's reading performance, and using only multiple-choice questions to assess reading or arithmetic skills would hardly be sensitive to how or why a child performed.

There are instances when diagnostic tests lose their diagnostic sensitivity by attempting to diagnose too much. The Keymath Diagnostic Arithmetic Test (Connolly, Nachtman, and Pritchett, 1971) consists of fourteen subtests and was standardized on children drawn from kindergarten through grade eight. This test has many subtests, but each subtest has a limited number of items. As an example, the addition computation subtest consists of fifteen problems ranging from primary facts (e.g., 1 + 3) to addition of fractions. There is absolutely no reason to believe that fifteen addition problems covering a grade span from kindergarten to grade eight will be able to provide "diagnostic" information; that is, information that will allow a test user to understand a child's specific strengths and weaknesses in addition computation. If a test developer feels that fourteen subtests are necessary, the number of items will have to be limited to make the test a manageable length. Cronbach (1970) referred to this as the bandwidth-fidelity dilemma. He stated that "attempting to capture rich detail by using many scores, each from a small sample of behavior, gets poor information" (p. 180). This is the nature of the bandwidth-fidelity dilemma: the greater the bandwidth (the more subtests) the less the fidelity (the number of items within a subtest). If a test maker devised a test consisting of 100 subtests, and each subtest consisted of a large number of items, the administration of this test would likely result in the mental and/or physical collapse of test giver and child. A diagnostic test that attempts to diagnose too much will generally offer little in the way of understanding in addition to giving the false impression that a child's performance had been diagnosed.

SUBTEST NAMES

A test will very often be comprised of a series of smaller tests or subtests. A reading test will include subtests measuring vocabulary, comprehension, sound discrimination; an arithmetic test will include subtests measuring addition, subtraction, word problems, measurement; a language test will include subtests measuring oral vocabulary, syntax, and expression. Subtests may not have the benefit of being named after a university, state or individual, but they do often exhibit a certain *savoir faire*. Spatial relationships, angels-in-the-snow (yes, indeed), ocular pursuits, nonsense words, numerical reasoning, auditory discrimination, picture arrangement, figure-ground, visual sequential memory, auditory reception, listening, receptive syntax, alphabet, auding, general information, spelling, form constancy, concepts, object assembly, word meaning, mazes — subtest names have a directness, a sense of purpose. This, however, does not mean that a subtest name must be ungarnished. The Wechsler Intelligence Scale for Children has a subtest that requires a child to arrange several pieces of cardboard (4 to 8 pieces) to form an object (e.g., a car). This puzzle task goes by the subtest name of object assembly. Object assembly is not a farfetched description (although actual objects are not assembled), and it does suggest greater "psychological" import than a subtest called puzzle completion or putting-together-cardboard-pieces-to-form-an-object.

Subtest names vary in the degree to which they embellish a task. The Wechsler Intelligence Scale for Children has another subtest called digit span. This task consists of a child repeating series of digits presented by an examiner (e.g., "3 − 8 − 6"). The Illinois Test of Psycholinguistic Abilities also has a subtest which consists of a child repeating a series of digits presented by an examiner (e.g., "5 − 2 − 8"). As contrasted to the mundane Wechsler subtest name (digit span), the Illinois Test of Psycholinguistic Abilities refers to its digit span subtest as "auditory sequential memory." The difference between intelligence and psycholinguistics is only a name apart.

The relation between a subtest name and the overall claim of what a test measures is usually, but not always, clear. Arithmetic subtests can be found on intelligence tests; intelligence-type subtests (e.g., auditory vocabulary, general information) can be found on achievement tests; just about anything might be thrown into a perceptual-motor test, while language tests and subtests are totally unpredictable. Regarding language subtests, a task might require a child to read and then select one of four sentences (e.g., Fred coming in first; Fred came in first; Fred come in first; Fred comed in first). This is one language skill, but to say that information obtained by such a subtest represented language usage, a likely subtest name, would be more than an exaggeration.

Not only can the relationship between subtests and tests be suspect, but specific subtest items can be the cause of much head scratching. The Vineland Social Maturity Scale (Doll, 1965) entails gathering "information obtained from someone intimately familiar with the person scored, such as the mother, the father . . ." (p. 8). Under the category of socialization (this test has categories and not subtests) one of the questions is whether a child "disavows" Santa Claus. The explanation given in the manual for scoring stated that "rejects anthropomorphic concept of Santa Claus intellectually, but may retain emotional or symbolic concept . . ." (p. 26). And from this we learn of a child's ability to socialize?

A test name is not synonymous with what a test measures, and a test user would be well advised to take a test name lightly and to thoughtfully assess what information a test or subtest might yield.

TEST NAME SELECTOR

Selecting a test name can be an intellectually trying task. The following, offered as a public service to budding test makers, should eliminate much of this frustration and anguish. Table XIX presents a procedure for selecting or generating test names. One entry is selected from each of the five columns. The first column allows the user to indicate his or her own name, to select a name that personifies honesty (e.g., Lincoln), to choose a name that connotes scholarship (e.g., Sorbonne, Harvard), or to incorporate a name that has not been previously used (e.g., North Dakota, Moscow). The selection of entries from the *type, class, area,* and *recipient* columns are self-explanatory and will depend on the type of test a person has in mind.

TABLE XIX

A PROCEDURE FOR GENERATING TEST NAMES

Proper Noun	*Type*	*Class*	*Area*	*Recipient*
Your name	Diagnostic	Inventory	of Language	for Adults
North Dakota	Screening	Test	of Reading	for Children
Harvard	Developmental	Profile	of Intelligence	for Infants
Sorbonne	Individual	Battery	of Achievement	for Males
Moscow	Attainment	Scale	of Learning	for Females
Lincoln	Sequential	Survey	of Arithmetic	for Everybody

Names such as the Lincoln Screening Scale of Intelligence for Everybody or the Harvard Sequential Survey of Language for Females will assuredly have great appeal to consumers of educational tests. However, an added tip to enhance the appeal of the name selected is to select a name which can be reduced to an acronym. Test makers have long known that a successful test rests just as much on a pithy abbreviation or designation as test content. A name such as the Moscow Individual Scale of Reading for Infants which could be designated the MISRI and pronounced "misery" would stand a better chance of being remembered, and therefore purchased, than a test name not as neologically endowed.

Test names—rapturous titles torn between ambiguity and possibility. . . .

"Exactly so," said Alice.
"Then you should say what you mean," the March Hare went on.
"I do," Alice hastily replied; "at least—at least I mean what I say—that's the same thing, you know."
"Not the same thing a bit!" said the Hatter. (Carroll, 1865)

Chapter Nine

MULTIPLE-CHOICE TESTS

MULTIPLE-CHOICE TASKS

W RITING MULTIPLE-CHOICE tests has become an art form in the United States. Unlike tests that result in varied responses (e.g., essay tests or evaluating a child's oral reading), thereby increasing the time and degree of subjectivity needed to evaluate a child's performance, multiple-choice tests reduce reality to a series of alternatives. The effect of this reduction is to produce tests that are economical, can be objectively scored, and discriminate among individuals. These factors have contributed to the use of multiple-choice tests in almost every phase of education and to the development of multiple-choice tests that are conceptually sound, often highly creative, and statistically pleasing.

Multiple-choice tests have been constructed to measure skill or aptitude in reading, mathematics, language, social sciences, natural sciences, medicine, college performance, art, law, and engineering. The appeal of multiple-choice items lies in the simplicity of form and construction. A question is asked, alternatives provided, and a response made. Multiple-choice items ranging in number from a few to over a hundred can be presented at a modest cost and responded to in a short period of time without digressions caused by unique or problematical responses. A multiple-choice test can be administered by one individual to extremely large groups, machine scored, and statistically analyzed with a minimum of time and effort. The result of this paper-pencil exercise in educational testing efficiency is a test that discriminates among individuals—some receive high scores, some average scores, and some low scores. With scores determined, children can be categorized, labels assigned, persons accepted or rejected, and decisions made. It is no wonder that multiple-choice tests reign supreme in educational testing.

One might argue whether multiple-choice items emerged shortly after the appearance of man, but the current multiple-choice item form is fairly well established in educational testing. A multiple-choice item has two basic components: a stem and a series of alternatives. The alternatives can be further subdivided into distracters or foils (i.e., wrong answers) and the correct answer. Most test makers use one correct answer or, if not correct, one best answer. The trick to succeeding on best-answer multiple choice tests is not to respond in terms of what the best answer is, or what you believe the best answer is, but what you believe the test maker believes the best answer is.

The first multiple-choice item shown in Figure 10 requires a child to match the stem (the letter *b*) to the second alternative. So as not to have a systematic arrangement of correct answers (e.g., alternative numer one is correct, then two, then three, then four, then one, etc.), test makers often use some type of randomization procedure to determine where correct answers will be placed. As an example, a random process (e.g., selecting numbers from a hat) might have resulted in the first question having the third alternative as the correct answer, the second question also having the third alternative as the correct answer, and the third question having the first alternative as the correct answer. The gist of all this is that if you ever take a technically sound multiple-choice test, and most standardized multiple-choice tests are, don't waste your time looking for a pattern of correct answers. However, if for a particular question the stem and alternatives have been checked for all possible clues and you still haven't the vaguest idea as to what the correct answer is, selecting an infrequently chosen alternative might not be such a bad idea. On a multiple-choice test, anything is better than blind guessing.

Unlike the first item, the second item in Figure 10 is presented by means of an oral stem ("Point to the cup.") and a child responds by pointing to the drawing which best represents the stimulus word (i.e., cup). The third item in Figure 10 has a pictorial stem and requires a child to match the initial sound in "shoe" with the first alternative. This item, as do the previous

LETTER MATCHING

b d b q h

AUDITORY VOCABULARY

BEGINNING SOUNDS

 sh ch su cu

Figure 10.   A sampling of multiple-choice questions.

two, consists of four alternatives. There is no rule stating how many alternatives should be used, but less than four will increase the possibiilty of guessing the correct response—the difference between right or wrong on a true and false test can be a flip of the coin. Although multiple-choice items with five alternatives are used, test makers are aware of the difficulty involved in constructing more than three or four alternatives that work; that is, that discriminate between low scoring and high scoring children.

GUESSING

The bane of every multiple-choice test maker is guessing. Items will occasionally be written that indicate the answer, as does the following by the article *an*:

HIS TRUNK WAS BIG.

AN——IS BIG.

A) ELEPHANT   B) WHALE   C) DINOSAUR   D) COW

Occasionally, information will be given in the stem that suggests the correct answer or suggests that a distracter is obviously wrong (e.g., before 1940 but after 1941); or the correct answer will be made too long (or too short) in comparison to the distracters. Overall, multiple-choice tests are quite sophisticated in countering the efforts of test-wise students. Such students are much more likely to profit on teacher-made tests, which are less rigorously constructed, than on standardized multiple-choice tests, which have been written in a homogeneous, thoughtful, style that would challenge the most persistent clue seeker.

However, there is the problem of guessing. Test makers cringe at the thought of an individual scoring high on a test as the result of guessing, out-and-out luck, or chance. No matter how little one knows or how remote the subject matter is, a test taker can always hope for a stupendous run of luck. Multiple-choice tests can be criticized for many reasons, but they do offer the unknowing test taker a much-needed glimmer of hope.

To guess or not to guess can be an important choice on a multiple-choice test. On a true and false test the probability of guessing a correct answer is 1 in 2, or 1/2, or .5. If there are 50 true-false items, and a person guessed at each answer, on the average a score of 25 would be expected ($50 \times .5 = 25$). On a test with four alternatives, the possibility of guessing a correct answer is 1 in 4, or 1/4, or .25. If there are 100 questions, on the average a score of 25 would be expected ($100 \times .25 = 25$).

To demonstrate the perils of multiple-choice testing, or multiple-choice guessing as it is known by some critics, a small experiment was conducted. A readiness subtest was administered to five individuals. The administration was different in that subjects (this is the terminology used when discussing individuals who participate in experiments) were requested to guess at each answer by indicating "one," "two," or "three." The Ss (this is the abbreviation used when discussing individuals who participate in experiments) were not told the stem or the alternatives, and the numbers elicited from each S signified the number of the alternative being guessed as correct. The subtest given consisted of 16 multiple-choice questions with each question having three alternatives. The probability of guessing a correct answer was 1 in 3 or .33, and a score of 5.3 ($16 \times .33 = 5.3$) was expected on the average. Several Ss thought this task peculiar, but all agreed to guess as specified.

Subject number one, a secretary, proved up to the task and managed to guess 9 correct answers. Subject number two, a four-year-old, guessed seven correct. This subject insisted upon using numbers other than one, two, and three as guesses but these numbers were not counted as actual responses. The last three subjects tested guessed 6, 3, and 9 correct answers.

The manual for the subtest indicated that a raw score between 8 and 10 is in the "average" range, a raw score between 4 and 7 is in the "low normal" range, and a raw score between 0 and 3 is in the "low" range. Using this information as a guideline, two individuals were in the average range, two in the low normal range, and one in the low range. Four of the subjects, when informed of their performance, were not at all impressed, while the four-year-old, after reaching ten for the third or fourth time, sensibly excused himself ("I don wanna play no more.") from further participation in the experiment—such are the ways of philosophical children. A final appraisal of the experiment indicated that guessing can distort scores, adults will submit to the most ridiculous tests, and children have more common sense than they are usually given credit.

In statistics, if there is a built-in bias or error in a method or procedure, a formula is developed to correct that bias or error. A traditional formula used to correct for guessing is as follows:

$$\text{NUMBER RIGHT} - \frac{\text{NUMBER WRONG}}{\text{NUMBER OF ALTERNATIVES} - 1}$$

The idea behind this formula is that the number of wrong answers will indicate the number of answers scored correctly by guessing. If a test consists of 100 items, and each item has four alternatives, on the average a child would guess 25 correct answers ($100 \times .25 = 25$). By the same token, 75 questions would be answered incorrectly. If a child answered 75 questions incorrectly, we could hypothesize that 25 items were answered correctly by guessing. The number of questions thought to be answered correctly by guessing can be found by dividing the number of wrong answers by the number of alternatives minus 1:

$$\frac{75}{4 - 1} = 25$$

Subtracting 25 (the number of questions thought to be answered correctly by guessing) from 25 (the number correct) results in a final score of 0.

If a test is comprised of 50 items, and each item has three alternatives, and a child received a score of 36, the number of questions thought to be answered correctly by guessing would be found as follows:

$$\frac{14}{3 - 1} = 7$$

The corrected score would be 36 (number correct) $- 7$ (correction factor), or 29. In other words, on a three alternative multiple-choice test, for every two wrong answers one answer is hypothesized to be answered correctly by guessing. If there are 14 incorrect answers, 7 answers are hypothesized to be correct as a result of guessing.

A formula that corrects for guessing would be very advantageous if it corrected for guessing. As it happens, an individual may guess but the guesses may be among three alternatives, or between two alternatives, but not invariably among all alternatives. Imagine a four alternative, 30 item multiple-choice test in which each item had one correct answer, one excellent distracter, and two alternatives that were obviously wrong. An individual could not differentiate between correct answers and excellent distracters, so responses to each item entailed guessing between two alternatives—one correct alternative and one incorrect alternative. In this situation, 15 items would be answered, on the average, correctly. Correcting for guessing would result in a final score of 10 ($15 - 15/3 = 10$). If this individual had been instructed not to guess, and these instructions had been followed, both corrected and uncorrected scores would be 0. There would be no wrong answers to estimate the number of items guessed correctly, but there would also be no correct items.

Still another possibility is an individual who chose the excellent distracter for each item. This person would seem to know something, but he would receive a score of 0 and a corrected score of -10 $(0 - 30/3 = -10)$. The possibility of this or the above example occurring is extremely unlikely, but it does serve to demonstrate that correcting for guessing may not always have the desired effect. For the test taker, irrespective of stern warnings to the contrary, eliminating what is wrong and guessing at what might be correct would seem appropriate behavior on multiple-choice tests.

The correction formula for guessing just described suggests that an individual can profit by not answering items. Using this reasoning, the problem of guessing can be dealt with by encouraging children to guess on all items. If all items are responded to by all children, the correction formula will not affect or change the rank ordering of final scores; that is, children will not benefit by not responding to items. This approach obviates the need for a correction formula and leaves only the problem of good guessing, bad guessing, and lucky guessing.

Yet another method for coping with guessing is to ignore the problem entirely. Children are told to respond as best they can, and each child is left to wrestle with the problem of whether to guess or not. This approach, although frequently used, does seem to benefit a child willing to take a risk more than a child inclined toward indecision or reticence.

In addition to estimating the number of answers guessed correctly, multiple-choice questions answered incorrectly can be used as a means for terminating testing. This is accomplished by determining a ceiling score—a point at which testing is discontinued because items are believed to be too difficult. This technique is often used on tests that are administered individually and that consist of items of increasing difficulty.

A ceiling is said to have been reached when a designated number of items have been answered incorrectly (e.g., 6 errors out of 8 consecutive responses, 5 errors out of 7 consecutive responses, 3 consecutive errors). An example of a ceiling level is shown in Table XX, where the scoring of a 15 item, 4 alternative multiple-choice test is presented. In this example, the criterion for a ceiling (the point at which testing stops) is 3 consecutive failures. Since items 8, 9, and 10 were failed consecutively, the ceiling score is 10. This means that items answered correctly below item 10 contribute to the final score, which in this case is 5, but that items above item 10 were not administered.

TABLE XX

EXAMPLE SHOWING CALCULATION OF CEILING SCORE FOR A
FIFTEEN ITEM MULTIPLE-CHOICE TEST

Item	Correct Alternative	Alternative Chosen
1	1	1
2	4	4
3	3	3
4	3	3
5	2	1 x
6	3	4 x
7	1	1
8	4	2 x
9	1	2 x
10	2	3 x
		———— Ceiling
11	1	
12	4	
13	3	
14	4	
15	2	

Determining a ceiling score is an efficient method for reducing testing time. Furthermore, a ceiling score may result in not subjecting a child to needless frustration by administering items that are far too difficult. On the other hand, a child's score might be depressed or inflated on the basis of several multiple-choice questions. No matter how much care is taken to arrange items according to item difficulty, guessing still exists, and determining a ceiling score can result in a child not being presented with questions to which he/she could respond correctly.

One thing is certain about multiple-choice questions: guessing is a problem.

DISCRIMINATION

The quality of a multiple-choice item is often determined by how well it discriminates among high scoring and low scoring individuals. If a test was administered to 100 persons, each item could be analyzed by comparing the choices of those who received the highest 30 percent of total test scores (high group) to those who received the lowest 30 percent of total test scores (low group).

	1	2*	3	4	0
HIGH GROUP	5	20	2	2	1
LOW GROUP	7	10	9	3	1

In this analysis the top row of numbers indicates the possible alternatives (0 signifies that an individual omitted answering that item), and the asterisk denotes the correct answer. As shown, 20 individuals from the high group answered this item correctly (the second alternative), as opposed to 10 individuals from the low group. Alternative number 3 appears to be a good distracter in that 9 individuals from the low group selected this as the correct answer.

Not all multiple-choice questions discriminate between high and low scoring individuals, as illustrated by the following item analysis:

	1	2	3	4*	0
HIGH GROUP	4	8	11	5	2
LOW GROUP	6	9	6	8	1

The wording of the item, general ambiguity, or simply an error in fact or conceptualization on the part of the item writer may have caused more low scoring individuals to select the correct answer (alternative number 4) than high scoring individuals. Of course, another possibility is that more low scoring persons knew the correct answer than high scoring persons. Although interesting, this possibility would be more informative than discriminatory—this item would be considered a bad item.

Discriminating among individuals is not inherently evil, as some would lead us to believe. There seems to be justification for discriminating among individuals on the basis of merit, performance, or effort. We are constantly being tested and evaluated in school, in our work, socially, athletically; discrimination on the basis of what we do or what we know is a fact of life. Even on a multiple-choice test, an item that discriminates among individuals can provide useful (i.e., diagnostic) information. The following item might indicate whether children confused plus and minus signs, combined components of the question to form an answer, or knew the primary addition fact.

$$\begin{array}{r} 7 \\ + 5 \\ \hline \end{array}$$ (A) 2   (B) 57   (C) 13   (D) 12

Multiple-choice items can provide useful information, but how often are multiple-choice tests analyzed to assess what is known or what has not been taught rather than solely to discriminate among individuals? Psychometricians glibly state that tests can provide vital feedback, but item performance on standardized multiple-choice tests is forever a mystery to most test takers. Providing such information would necessitate the development of massive item pools and new test production techniques—a prospect that might benefit test takers but is not in concert with the business aspects of developing and distributing tests.

Discriminating among individuals may be a democratic goal, but educational tests, and especially multiple-choice tests, discriminate with dubious results. Discriminating between low scoring and high scoring persons is a trivial case. Would not one expect high scoring persons to select more correct answers than low scoring persons? The important questions to be answered pertain to what it means to discriminate among individuals, what a test measures, and how a test corresponds to reality. Is the multiple-choice form to be considered the paradigm of reality? Can the complexity of what a person knows or how a person will perform be reduced to a series of alternatives, fixed and unbending?

An ominous turn of events in multiple-choice testing is the drop in quantitative and verbal test scores on college entrance tests. One prestigious group cited a decrease in reading and writing skills as being partially responsible for the decline in scores. As it is, the very tests used to suggest a decline in these skills, multiple-choice tests, are hardly absolute measures of reading or writing performance. Requiring a child to read (orally) or to write (other than completing an IBM scoring form) are not unheard-of methods for evaluating reading or writing.

Hoffmann (1962), in a book titled *The Tyranny of Testing,* argued that multiple-choice tests are not sensitive to individual interpretations. He stressed "how important it is to train students to organize their own thoughts and to put something of themselves into a project, and how damaging it can be to reward them for merely picking wanted answers at rates up to a hundred an hour" (p. 216). As logical and humane as this reasoning might be, experts in educational testing do not take kindly to criticism. Adkins (1974) appraised Hoffman's view of testing tyranny by stating that "this book presents detailed critiques of objective items that had appeared in published tests, often deducing what seem to be farfetched lines of reasoning" (p. 134). Although the exact meaning of Adkin's denouncement is somewhat cryptic, Hoffman did seem to overemphasize only one deficiency of testing (multiple-choice items). This was unfortunate, especially in view of the many other limitations, abuses, and misinterpretations prevalent in educational testing.

Opinions regarding multiple-choice tests are diverse, but there is no denying that they are cost-effective and discriminate among individuals. This efficiency does not mean that some children are not penalized, that important information is not overlooked, or that some children are not actually discriminated against; but only that low and high scoring children are discriminated between at a relatively low cost.

Children have the capacity to learn, to be motivated, and to create. These are not always of foremost concern when a multiple-choice test is constructed or administered.

Chapter Ten

IDENTIFYING AND CREATING PROBLEMS

CAUSATION

To MANY USERS, standardized tests provide a means for understanding a child, for determining why a child is not performing as expected, and for ascertaining a child's educational needs. The initial intent of testing may be altruistic—to help a child, to provide the most appropriate educational environment—but the effects of classifying a child, of delineating a specific cause for a child's performance can be misleading and educationally harmful.

The logic of using and interpreting educational tests is not always the epitome of truth and valid reasoning. This is partly exemplified by the use of so-called tests of intelligence to categorize children. Syllogistically, the reasoning is as follows:

TEST X MEASURES IQ.
JOHN SCORED LOW ON TEST X.
JOHN HAS A LOW IQ.

In this example the reasoning is impeccable, that is, if one accepts the premise that one test or that a single score can capture the complexities of an individual's intelligence. A truthful elaboration of the major premise would be something like this:

TEST X MEASURES WHAT MANY OTHER TESTS
   MEASURE.
JOHN SCORED LOW ON TEST X.
JOHN HAS A LOW IQ.

Resurrecting truth in the major premise would solve one problem, but another would be created in that the reasoning would no longer be valid—the conclusion could no longer be drawn that John has a low IQ.

Deducing that a child has low intelligence may mimic one phase of scientific inquiry, but as long as the premise is in error, the conclusion (categorizing a child as having low intelligence) will not be far behind. What frequently happens is that when a child does not perform as expected, determining the cause (deducing low intelligence as the reason for a child's behavior) is equated with helping a child. This quasi-medical approach to remediation (find the cause, cure the patient) might be of some benefit if a child did profit. What usually happens, however, is that the cause quickly becomes a stigma, and a child eases into a pattern of ostracism, reduced expectations, and inferior programming.

Low intelligence is an example of a general cause, but tests can also be used to identify specific causes. A typical deduction might be as follows:

SOME CHILDREN WITH LEARNING PROBLEMS
   SCORE LOW ON TASK X.
JOHN SCORED LOW ON TASK X.
JOHN HAS A LEARNING PROBLEM.

To make this syllogism valid, "children with learning problems" would have to be changed to "only children with learning problems." As it now stands, one could not deduce that John has a learning problem—the possibility exists that children without learning problems also score low task X or that children with learning problems do not score low on task X. All this, of course, is dependent on being able to accurately diagnose children with learning problems.

Of the myriad tasks in educational testing, perceptual-motor tests have been used extensively to ferret out specific causative factors. Several commonly used perceptual-motor tasks are presently in Figure 11. The first task is a figure-ground item in which an individual must discriminate the figure from the background (slanted lines). The second task requires a child to draw a line between the two horizontal lines. The third task entails the simultaneous drawing of circles. For a right-handed person, the right-hand circle should be counter-clockwise and the left-hand circle should be clockwise. The last task is a multiple-choice matching of identical geometric shapes.

FIGURE-GROUND

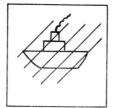

LEFT-RIGHT LINE DRAWING

DRAWING CIRCLES SIMULTANEOUSLY

MATCHING COMPLETE FIGURES

Figure 11.   The creative world of perceptual-motor tasks.

To demonstrate how an innocuous perceptual-motor task can be used to identify the cause of a child's learning problem, and thereby indicate what remedial action should be taken, consider the following example. On the basis of teacher ratings, two groups of children were identified: achievers and nonachievers. Children in each group were then given a figure-ground test (see Fig. 11). The tests were scored and the following table constructed to show the relationship between figure-ground performance and achievement. The pass-fail entry indicates ability or inability to distinguish a figure from distracting background stimuli.

	ACHIEVER	NONACHIEVER
PASS	40	10
FAIL	10	40

In this example, the achiever and nonachiever groups each consisted of 50 children. For the achievers, 40 passed the figure-ground test and 10 failed. For the nonachiever group, 10 passed the figure-ground test and 40 failed. These data show a relationship between figure-ground performance and achievement, but one could not deduce that poor figure-ground ability was the cause of low achievement. The fact remains that some achievers also failed the figure-ground test; but more important, there is absolutely no way of knowing whether low achievement was caused by poor figure-ground abiilty, or whether low achievement and poor figure-ground ability were both caused by a third, unidentified factor. The generalization that nonachievers score low on figure-ground tasks in no way permits an individual to claim that figure-ground performance can be used to specify the cause of a child's academic difficulties.

In the manual for the *Developmental Test of Visual Perception,* Frostig, Lefever and Whittlesey (1966) stated that "identification and training of children with visual perceptual disabilities during the preschool years or at the time of school entrance would help prevent many instances of school failure and maladjustment caused by visual perceptual difficulties" (p. 6). There is just no way of knowing, based on an observed relationship between achievement and a task or group of tasks, whether one was caused by the other. An argument could be developed that poor figure-ground performance was actually caused by nonachievement. In the long run this type of reasoning might actually profit a child in that time would be spent developing achievement-related skills and not subjecting a child to meaningless perceptual-motor training.

The finding that "the test scores of some children tend to be high, while the test scores of some children tend to be low" affords considerable creative flexibiilty when devising tasks to show what causes a child's perceived problem. Delacato (1966) stated that "the diagnosis of a reading problem, therefore, becomes an evaluation of the state of Neurological Organization" (p. 5). This is based on the premise that reading problems are caused by a lack of neurological organization. Delacato's method for diagnosing neurological organization includes assessing handedness, footedness, eyedness, cross-pattern walking, creeping, and a child's sleeping position. He cautioned that "children who are well organized at this level sleep in a prone position and in a homolateral pattern" (p. 22). Having assumed that the task is the cause, Delacato stated that "if the child fails any test at any single level, his Neurological Organization is not complete" and that "treatment follows the diagnostic program . . ." (p. 23). Teaching a child to creep *properly* may not be harmful, but this does seem to be carrying creative license to its limit. Poor readers are poor creepers, therefore poor creeping causes poor reading—a questionable generalization, faulty reasoning, and how a child can be helped is decided.

TEST PROFILES

Although a test may not specify a cause, how test information is presented may give the impression that all possible causes have been investigated. This is accomplished by visually depicting a child's test performance by means of a test profile. Figure 12 shows an achievement profile in which the shaded area indicates average performance and the circled numbers represent stanines received on each of the four subtests. An achievement profile gives the impression of describing a child's academic performance and clearly explaining areas of "normal" and "below normal" work.

Figure 13 illustrates a psychological profile. In this example, the eight subtests that comprised the test are indicated by abbreviations (e.g., Vo indicates vocabulary, Di represents digit span). The mean of each subtest is 10 and the standard deviation is 3. The psychological profile gives the impression that a child's psychological processes have been assessed and, as a result, specific deficiencies or meaningful patterns can be designated. The profile gives the impression of something more than a series

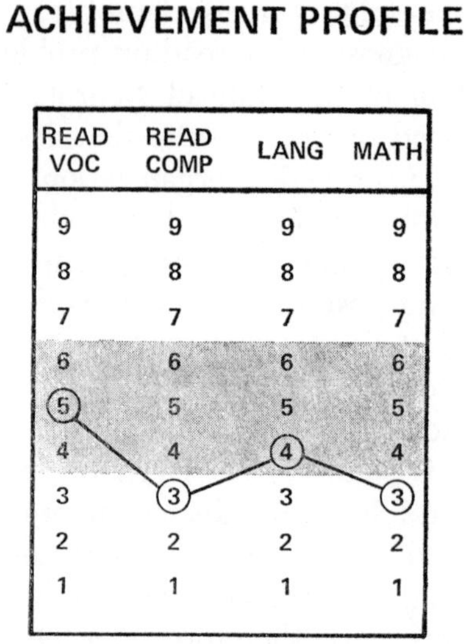

ACHIEVEMENT PROFILE

READ VOC	READ COMP	LANG	MATH
9	9	9	9
8	8	8	8
7	7	7	7
6	6	6	6
⑤	5	5	5
4	4	④	4
3	③	3	③
2	2	2	2
1	1	1	1

Figure 12.   An example of an achievement test profile.

of tests and isolated tasks that may only give a faint glimpse of a child's psychological processes.

The last example shows how a meaningful theoretical relationship can be misrepresented by a test profile. Three subtest scores are shown in Figure 14: language reception, language association, and language expression. Assume that the first test was comprised of questions that required a "yes" or "no" response, the second test consisted of discerning relationships (e.g., "In what way is an apple like a pear?"), and the third test entailed describing how different objects are used ("What can you do with a brick?"). The mean of each subtest is 50 and the standard deviation is 10. In the psycholinguistic profile shown in Figure 14, a score of 45 was received in reception, a score of 30 in association, and a score of 60 in expression.

When an individual processes information, an assumption can be made that information is processed in discrete steps. First an individual receives the information, the information is then related (associated) with past experiences, and finally an individual can relate or express information that has been received and stored. Examples of receptive processes preceding expres-

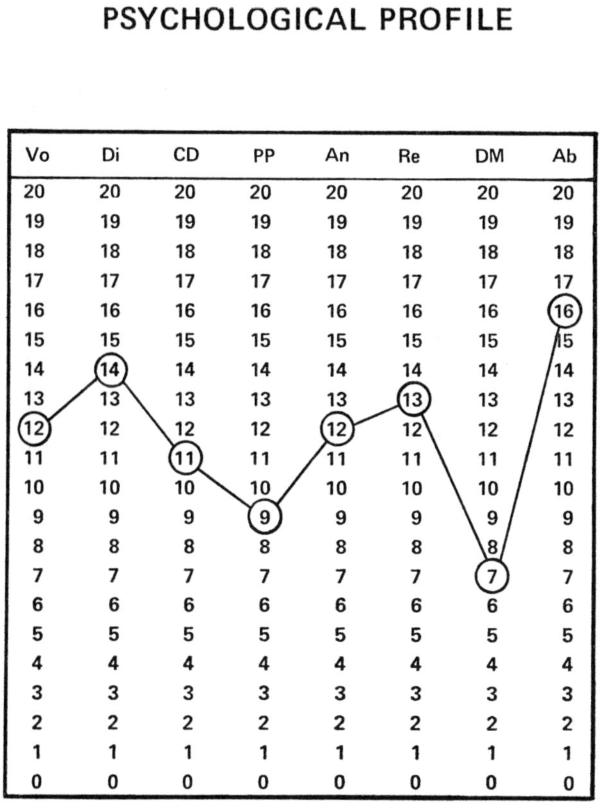

PSYCHOLOGICAL PROFILE

Vo	Di	CD	PP	An	Re	DM	Ab
20	20	20	20	20	20	20	20
19	19	19	19	19	19	19	19
18	18	18	18	18	18	18	18
17	17	17	17	17	17	17	17
16	16	16	16	16	16	16	(16)
15	15	15	15	15	15	15	15
14	(14)	14	14	14	14	14	14
13	13	13	13	13	(13)	13	13
(12)	12	12	12	(12)	12	12	12
11	11	(11)	11	11	11	11	11
10	10	10	10	10	10	10	10
9	9	9	(9)	9	9	9	9
8	8	8	8	8	8	8	8
7	7	7	7	7	7	(7)	7
6	6	6	6	6	6	6	6
5	5	5	5	5	5	5	5
4	4	4	4	4	4	4	4
3	3	3	3	3	3	3	3
2	2	2	2	2	2	2	2
1	1	1	1	1	1	1	1
0	0	0	0	0	0	0	0

Figure 13. A typical psychological test profile.

sive processes include understanding speech and speaking, and reading and writing.

The profile shown in Figure 14 appears so descriptive that a test user might easily forget that the tests mentioned may not measure reception, association, and expression, or that the tasks mentioned are trite examples of reception, association, and expression, or that each of the three subtests might measure reception, association, and expression. The profile removes a test user from these possibilities and creates a fanciful image of language processes.

A test profile appears to mirror reality—limits of achievement are defined, all possible areas of intellectual development are

PSYCHOLINGUISTIC PROFILE

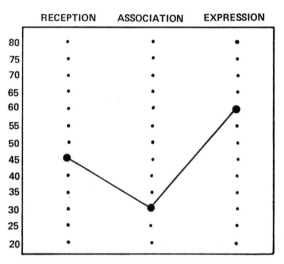

Figure 14.   A language profile.

labeled, logical components of language are specified. In most instances, there is no way of knowing what subtests are important or if an essential subtest has been ignored. The mere fact that an area has been identified and subtest scores arranged in a seemingly all-embracing profile does not give credence to individual subtests or that comparisons between subtests are at all meaningful. A profile may be aesthetic, and a test maker may believe in the reality of a profile, but meaning and usefulness are more than labels, scores, and a series of connecting lines.

SEARCHING FOR ANSWERS AND MYTHS

Whenever test scores are used to imply causation, the possibility of shallow or circular reasoning exists. A test is used to show that a child has low intelligence. The actual reasoning is similar to saying that a child has a low test score (e.g., achievement test score) as a result of a low test score (e.g., IQ test score).

Searching for a cause need not stop with a test score. Jensen

(1969) hypothesized that genetic factors may account for differences between the IQ test scores of black and white children. No matter how many correlations are calculated, or how many correlations evaluated, the possibility still exists that test score differences (which are not to be confused with intellectual differences) can be explained by factors other than genetic differences (e.g., discrimination).

When a child is not behaving as expected or a child's academic performance is below average, the assumption is invariably made that something must be wrong with the child. The possibility that something is wrong with the teacher, program, or school or that nothing is wrong is rarely considered. In the field of special education a category has been created that permits a child's "problem" to be identified without having the slightest idea what the problem is or whether the problem is real or imaginary. This is accomplished by first defining the categories in which a child can be placed (e.g., mentally retarded, speech impaired, hearing impaired, visually handicapped, orthopedically handicapped). As it happens, children cannot always be neatly (or legally) categorized so that a great many children with "problems" have not had the cause of their difficulties identified. This has been solved by creating a final category that includes all those not belonging to already defined categories. As an example, if we call this final category "learning disabilities," and we assume that all children who are believed to have problems can be categorized (i.e., a cause for their behavior can be identified), and a child does not belong to existing categories, then the child must be a member of a final or last category; the child is learning disabled.

All children have the right to an educational program that will best maximize their interests and skills. This, however, does not mean that a child should be the subject of the following dialogue:

"What's wrong with Bobby?"
"He has a reading problem."
"What's his problem?"
"He's learning disabled."
"Why's he learning disabled?"
"He has a reading problem."

Identifying a cause for a physical ailment will usually indicate the most appropriate and effective medical intervention. This is not always the case in education. For many children classified as educable mentally retarded (children with IQ scores approximately between 50 and 80) the resulting educational intervention (placing a child in a class with other children said to be retarded) is often less effective than no special remedial programming whatsoever (see Johnson, 1962).

In some instances the cause identified is so trivial and/or obscure that treating the cause is educationally worthless. A practitioner, well intentioned and hard working, may believe that improving a child's digit span, ability to walk a balance beam, or creeping skill is the essence of remediation, but surely a child deserves better than the training of isolated "test" skills.

If specifying a cause is often questionable, the resulting remediation specified would seem just as pointless. Interestingly enough, this is not always the case. Assume that the cause of a child's unacceptable academic behavior was said to be an inability to move, while lying down, designated body parts (e.g., "Move your right arm and left leg."). The relationship between this skill and academic achievement might be tenuous, but the effects of increased attention, verbal interaction, and improved motivation on the part of the child may serve to promote academic performance. Naturally, the possibility of this occurring decreases as meaningful educational activities are replaced by esoteric psychometric tasks.

A frequent tactic by test users is to drag out a barrage of statistics to "prove" the worth of testing and remedial procedures. Numbers, being numbers, are easily misinterpreted, distorted, or molded to support just about any hypothesis, theory, or preposterous idea. To pronounce a reading program effective because the mean grade equivalent of a group of third graders increased from 3.0 to 3.9 after one full school year would ignore other possible causative factors (e.g., the teacher, other classroom activities, normal student progress, home activities). If a different reading program had been used, the final mean grade equivalent might have been 4.9 instead of 3.9.

Another example of questionable statistics involves the phenomenon of test scores regressing toward the mean. A situation is shown in Table XXI in which 10 children were classified into two groups on the basis of a 10 item language test. A test given prior to a remedial program or intervention is referred to as a pretest. Children with the 5 highest scores were assigned to the high group, and children with the 5 lowest scores were assigned to the low group. A two month remedial program was implemented for children in the low language group. The 10 item language test was then administered to both groups of children a second time (posttest).

TABLE XXI

EXAMPLE OF REGRESSION TOWARD THE MEAN

Group	Child	Pretest	Posttest
	Lefty	10	9
	Louie	9	10
High	Homer	8	5
	Jane	7	7
	Fred	6	3
		Mean = 8.0	Mean = 6.8
	Tulip	5	8
	Nancy	4	4
Low	Mary	3	6
	Gunther	2	1
	Herman	1	2
		Mean = 3.0	Mean = 4.2

Pretest and posttest means were calculated for children in both low and high language groups. A comparison of low group means revealed that the mean language score increased from 3.0 to 4.2. Just the opposite of this, the mean language score for the high group decreased from 8.0 to 6.8. Do these data show that the language intervention was effective? No! Although high, the correlation between pretest and posttest scores is not perfect. The actual correlation between pretest and posttest scores is 0.789. For some children luck and circumstance acted to maximize pretest scores, while for other children these factors combined to produce low pretest scores. These inequities evened out somewhat on the posttest, thus causing low group language scores to increase and high group language scores to decrease.

As a final example of how regression toward the mean can

be interpreted as a meaningful finding, the posttest scores in Table XXI were classified into two groups: children with high posttest scores (Louie, Lefty, Tulip, Jane, and Mary) and children with low posttest scores (Homer, Nancy, Fred, Herman, and Gunther). The mean score for the 5 children with high posttest scores is 8.0, and the mean score for the 5 children with the lowest posttest scores is 3.0. A further analysis revealed that the pretest mean of the 5 children with high posttest scores is 6.8, and that the mean pretest score of the 5 children with low posttest scores is 4.2. Have children with high posttest scores benefited more from language remediation than children with low posttest scores? Or have children with low pretest scores benefited more from language remediation than children with high pretest scores? In all likelihood what has been demonstrated is that high scoring children tend to score somewhat lower when retested, and that low scoring children tend to score somewhat higher when retested.

Regression phenomena: children who received the highest scores on one test did not receive the highest scores on all other tests; children with the highest IQ scores will not always have the highest achievement scores; children with the lowest reading scores will not always have the lowest arithmetic scores.

If a researcher was trying to establish support for a new academic program, grouping children on the basis of low and high scores, administering the program, and then retesting would likely result in greater gains by the children initially assigned to the low group. Of course, the opposite would likely occur for the children in the high group (their gains would likely be lower) but someone setting about "to establish support for" or "to prove the effects of" a program surely would conveniently overlook something as dreary and lifeless as regression effects.

Searching for a cause is never an easy undertaking, and rather than developing lucid insights into why children behave, we stumble over our own biases, expectations, and doctrinaire beliefs.

Chapter Eleven

MOTIVATION

THE APPEAL AND REWARD OF TEST TAKING

IF EDUCATIONAL TESTS could be evaluated solely on physical appearances, testing would be a smashing success. One test stresses the colorfulness of its materials and assures the test user that the test was designed to be motivating. There is no way of knowing whether a child was ever asked if this test were interesting or motivating—and probably with good reason since children can be too candid.

The actual appeal of a test is, for the most part, conjecture, but there is no doubt that the advertisements for educational tests are attractive and inviting. The contents of a test are colorfully photographed. Bits and pieces, puzzles and beads, tapes and puppets, and forms and manuals are prominently displayed, tempting and tantalizing, evoking images of use much like toys in a Christmas catalog. There are also colored stills of examiners testing and children being tested. The examiners have expressions of understanding and deep compassion, and the children seem enthused, determined, not wanting to miss the opportunity of having been tested.

If the pictorial descriptions are not sufficient inducements, the accompanying verbiage can be irresistible. Is the test reliable? Why of course it's reliable. Is the test valid? Why of course the test is valid. Can the test be administered quickly? Of course—in thirty minutes, or fifteen minutes, or five minutes. But is the test expensive? A pittance, a mere pittance: the complete kit is only $33.95, scoring forms (pkg/50) are $4.50, the manual is $3.00, technical manual $2.50, answer key $.50, specimen kit $40.00, and for the heavy user there is always the deluxe edition, which sells for the low, low price of. . . .

Educational tests are designed to be attractive to persons who purchase tests. In the development of a test the actual motivation considered is the motivation of a test user to complete and return an order form.

Educational tests can be used to make a decision (e.g., grouping children, admitting individuals to special programs) or as a device to motivate persons to learn. A test could be made up of the most dull and insipid questions imaginable, but a child might still be motivated to put forth a concentrated effort because of the perceived consequences. On the topic of motivation and testing Adkins (1974) made the following observations:

> Another very significant purpose of tests in the classroom, one that warrants further extension, is as a direct aid in motivation and thus in teaching. Students who know they are to be tested often will do more studying and learn more than would otherwise be the case. Cramming for the purpose of passing a test with no intent to remember beyond it is poor practice. Nevertheless, even this approach to learning undoubtedly results in more knowledge than would no studying at all. (p. 10)

Although these remarks are directed more toward classroom tests than standardized tests, they do represent a common attitude concerning the motivational qualities of educational tests: children will be motivated to learn or achieve in order to obtain acceptable test scores. This is contrary to the philosophy that a child will learn because the material is interesting, or because the teacher is interesting, or because of a healthy curiosity, but using a test as a scare tactic can be an effective method for increasing test scores.

Although some children learn at an early school age that high test scores are rewarded and low test scores are punished, many children must endure educational testing without either a conscious or subconscious awareness of this age-old educational dictum. For some children the problem is a matter of an over-rational and unidimensional approach to reality. If a teacher is boring, a rational behavior would be to ignore the teacher. If material presented is boring, a logical alternative would be to ignore the material. What is worth noting is that average or near average test performance for some children is short of being miraculous considering the manner in which "learning" was conducted.

Should a learning environment be less than stimulating for a child, or should a child find a particular learning environment less than stimulating, the final interpretation of educational test scores will not be influenced. A child receives a score; a child is responsible for his or her own test scores, and the possibility that a child had no earthly reason to ingest a body of information does not signify exoneration for poor test performance. The burden of responsibility is placed with the child so that a child not tolerant of boredom or tedium is at a decided disadvantage.

If a test is to be a motivating force (i.e., good performance will be rewarded and/or poor performance will be punished), a child's lack of interest in the material to be evaluated cannot overshadow the consequences of having been evaluated. Every child probably has a limit as to the pedagogical nonsense that can be endured under the threat of being tested and graded.

For very young children there is no need to use tests as motivational crutches. Small children are moderately agreeable, and if told to attend, learn, or memorize, they will generally perform as best they can. But for the child who does not try, what good are threats? How effective would it be to say, "Herman, if you don't learn your letters and pass the test, you'll flunk kindergarten?" Test results are important to test users, and only as a child grows older and an interest in learning is slowly replaced by an interest in doing well on tests will test results motivate an individual to learn; that is, if studying for a test is equated with the proverbial read-test-forget syndrome and not learning in the nobler sense.

There are innumerable motivational factors that can affect a child's test performance. At the time of testing the examiner can play a role in how a child will perform. What do young children think during their first group testing when their teacher is transformed into TEST EXAMINER and soberly announces, "Now you know what to do. I don't want any talking, and I can't give any more help. Are you ready?" The ending question is, as you can well imagine, rhetorical. For some, testing children provides an opportunity to demonstrate their authority: "Clear your desks! No talking! When I say stop, stop!" The authoritarian atmosphere of group testing might petrify a few, raise the anxiety level of some, and not affect the majority to any great extent—most children do have a surprising amount of grit.

The instructions for group tests are often excessively rigid to insure that examiners do not omit important information or provide too much information (such as the answers to the test). In group testing the regimentation of instructions, procedures, and materials is more important than creating optimal conditions under which a child could be assessed. The primary goal of group testing is not an insightful evaluation of a child, but the administration of an identical test so that children can be compared with one another.

Group testing can affect a child's test performance, but so can individual testing. Wechsler (1949) stated that "much damage has been done to testing programs in the schools by examiners who were too engrossed in administering tests to show a personal interest in the individual child . . ." and "if a personal relationship cannot be maintained the test results may measure, indirectly, the examiner's lack of sensitivity, and do the subjects an injustice if the scores are used for school placement or other administrative purposes" (p. 21). Children are sensitive, and a careless remark or frown can be as ruinous as not selecting the correct test answers.

A test yields a score or group of scores. What a test does not report is whether a child was preoccupied, or whether a child was hungry, or whether a child was excessively anxious. A test might be administered under proletarian conditions, but to a child a set of multiple-choice questions might be insignificant when compared to the task of surviving school, street, or family.

TESTING AND FEEDBACK

An important dimension of tests is their capacity to provide feedback. A test was given, answers responded to, and final scores diligently calculated. When returned, an individual can profit from knowing what was answered correctly or incorrectly and why certain answers were correct or incorrect. If the test giver is a reasonable individual, specific test questions can be dickered about, and individual interpretations of specific questions or answers offered.

Educational tests, the standardized type, are not generally used to provide adequate feedback; more important, they are often used with duplicity and disregard for individual rights. Test authorities openly admit that IQ scores can be misunderstood, that achievement scores (e.g., grade equivalents) can be misleading, and sundry derived scores and percentiles can be mistakingly interpreted as unquestionable scientific indices of academic behavior. Rather than minimizing these deficiencies. test specialists and users have adhered to a plan of concealment. If IQ scores will be misunderstood, don't report IQ scores; if test scores will be misinterpreted, bury them in normal curves and linear transformations.

Would a child's preparation for a test or performance on a test be different if the consequences for good or poor test performance were previously announced? A child's entire academic career could depend on a single readiness test or test that was said to measure IQ. What would happen if children were told that "if your IQ score is less than 80, you can't go to school with your peers and you'll be placed in a program that has a hodgepodge curriculum and where learning is more the result of luck than design?"

Naturally, informing a child of the consequences of being tested is impractical. The anxiety this would cause children would be barbaric. And how would an IQ that is not an intelligence quotient be explained? The problem is further confounded by the fact that many test users are not sure how test information will be used. A child may not be capable of being aware of why he is being tested or how the results will be used; however, parents, teachers, and all those in a position to act as advocate should know exactly how a child is to be tested, why a child is to be tested, and how results are to be used. Children must be protected from an unfeeling and reckless use of test scores. This can only be accomplished by scrutiny and vigilance, and by not being duped by the reported importance or meaningfulness of a test or score.

If a test cannot be used to help a child, if a test cannot provide feedback, then the test is worthless from a child's point of view—and calling a child retarded or assigning a child to the vulture reading group is not to be misconstrued as help. All too often, tests are given with the primary aim of classification. The feedback, if it can be called that, is in the form of admitting or denying, placing or not placing, passing or failing. As an example, IQ tests are often given to determine if a child can be legally placed in a class for the "retarded" and not to further delineate meaningful psychological or educational strategies.

One fallacy perpetuated by professionals is that decisions are best left with the professionals. Because decisions can be momentous, tests are bathed in secrecy to insure that all children have a "fair" chance. Because test consequences can be far reaching, test administration is rigid and closely monitored to prevent desperate acts (copying multiple-choice markings) by desperate persons. Because test results can be misinterpreted, scores are withheld or presented in a deceptive manner. An administrator scoffs at a test score, claims that it is only a number, and then uses that very score to categorize a child.

If a test is given, it should provide useful information and not meaningless indices and incomprehensible scores. Where educational tests are concerned, there is no substitute for scrutiny, vigilance, and constant questioning.

TEACHER EXPECTATIONS

The effects of a test score do not end with a decision or reporting of results. There has been a controversy in education as to whether knowledge of a child's test performance will influence how that child is treated. If a teacher knew that a child's IQ score was high, would student-teacher interaction be of a lesser quality than if the child's IQ was said to be low?

In 1968, Robert Rosenthal and Lenore Jacobson published a book entitled *Pygmalion in the Classroom*. These authors described a research project that was designed to determine if teacher expectations could affect a child's performance on a test of intelligence. Children from eighteen classes were administered an IQ test, which yielded three IQ scores: total IQ, reasoning IQ, and verbal IQ. At the beginning of the school year, following the testing, teachers were told that 20 percent of the children had been identified as "potential spurters." That is, these children were predicted to show "dramatic" gains in intellectual development. In actuality the 20 percent identified as spurters were selected at random. As the authors stated, "the difference between the special children and the ordinary children, then, was only in the mind of the teacher" (p. 175).

The results of this experiment revealed that children expected to gain or evidence a spurt in intellectual development did indeed show an increase in IQ scores when tested a second time. One of the experimental (spurter) groups, a second grade group comprised of six students, had a pretest total IQ mean of 113 and a posttest total IQ mean of 136—a difference of 23 IQ score points. It should be noted that pretests were given prior to telling teachers how children were expected to perform.

The results of this project suggested that a teacher's expectation of a child's ability based on IQ did affect how a teacher reacted to a student. The authors of this study reported that teachers adopted a self-fulfilling prophecy: behavior was exhibited that reinforced an initial prediction. If a teacher believed that a child had a low IQ, she would react to the child in a way perceived as appropriate for low IQ children.

The road to research is never smooth. Robert Thorndike (1968), in the *American Educational Research Journal,* indicated several misgivings about the Rosenthal and Jacobson project. He initiated his review of their research by stating that "alas, it is so defective technically that one can only regret that it ever got beyond the eyes of the original investigator! Though the volume may be an effective addition to educational propagandizing, it does nothing to raise the standards of educational research" (p. 708). Thorndike went on to note several interesting findings reported by Rosenthal and Jacobson. For instance, mean pretest reasoning IQ scores for three first grade classes were said to be 91, 47, and 31! A first grade class in a regular school system might be below average but a mean IQ of 31 is difficult to take seriously.

Rosenthal and Jacobson had a good idea. Telling a teacher that a child is not very bright or that a child is bright will probably affect how the teacher interacts with that child. If a teacher is presented with documentation that a child is retarded or slow, such as an IQ score, there is no reason to believe that expectations would not be lowered or that a child's true potential would not be ignored.

We have been brainwashed to believe that a score on a test, an IQ score, represents the intellectual capacity of a child. No matter how much we read to the contrary, no matter how often we rant that an IQ score is but a score on a test, as long as we tolerate a child's intelligence to be characterized by a single score, our perception of that child and our expectations for that child will be affected.

Children are really very intelligent. They can sense when they are held in low esteem, when they are alone, and when they have no one to be close to. They know what it means to be avoided, to have no one who cares what you do, and to become so hardened that you no longer feel like crying.

Rosenthal and Jacobson had a good idea, but they had to prove it by numbers. The moral of their pygmalion study is that what you say about a child can have far-reaching effects, and you should not publish suspicious statistics.

Chapter Twelve

TRUTH AND TESTING

RELIABILITY

ALTHOUGH RELIABILITY and validity are the cornerstones of educational testing, they are easily confused. Reliability refers to consistency or repeatability of test scores; validity concerns the meaning of test scores. If a test were constructed that entailed measuring the height of each person evaluated, and scores were used as an index of intelligence or to suggest an individual's intellectual potential, the resulting scores would be reliable but hardly valid. They would be reliable in the sense that the heights of persons measured were probably accurate; they would not be valid because a person's height would be a simpleminded index of intelligence.

A test can be reliable and not valid, but a test cannot be unreliable and valid. Translated, this means that a test can be accurate and meaningless, but a test cannot be inaccurate and meaningful. If a child responded randomly on a true and false test, a second testing, where responses were also random, would likely result in a different total test score. If test scores are inconsistent, if test scores are greatly affected by errors of measurement, then test reliability will be low.

Because the reliability of a test is reported as being high (or "acceptable"), this does not in the least suggest that the test is useful or that test scores are meaningful. Test reliability is a necessary but not sufficient condition for a psychometrically favorable evaluation of a test. A test might flaunt reliability statistics, but a test that does not measure what it purports to measure is still a bad test.

Test makers often use reliability coefficients to establish the dignity and integrity of a test. A test might measure an inconsequential trait, the norms might be primitive, the scores misleading, but if the test is reliable many test makers and users are more than satisfied. Nunnally (1967) stated that "a large proportion of journal articles on psychological measurement and a major portion of some books on the topic have been devoted to measurement error. This is probably because the theory of measurement error is so neatly expressable in mathematical terms, in contrast to some other important issues, e.g., validity, where grounds for argument are not so straightforward" (p. 173). Reliability is fairly easy to establish, it provides impressive statistics, and it can be used to promote a test. What more could a test maker want?

There are an endless number of factors that can affect a person's score on a test. A child might be sick, the room too hot, the examiner frightening, the questions ambiguous, the child is hungry, or the child has an unlucky run of guesses. These are just some of the factors that can produce errors of measurement.

A test score reflects specific knowledge at a specific time. On a 25 item vocabulary test a child received a score of 15. If 25 different vocabulary items had been selected, the child's score might have been 10, or 14, or 19. Furthermore, a second testing might reveal a score higher or lower than the first test score.

The purpose of reliability is to determine to what extent errors of measurement affect test scores. A commonly used method to describe test scores is to say that every score on a test is comprised of a true component and an error component so that

$$\text{TEST SCORE} = \text{TRUE SCORE} + \text{ERROR SCORE}$$

Although some might believe that a person's true score on a test is the score received, most scores are affected by errors of measurement.* If a test score is used to indicate a child's

---

* If a test were completely unreliable, the best estimate of a child's true score would be the test mean; there would be no reason to place faith in an obtained score. The lower the reliability of a test, the more an estimated true score will approach the test mean. A brief example will show how an estimated true score is found. If the mean of a test was 100, the reliability .90 and a

vocabulary, and vocabulary test items were poorly selected, scores from this test will not be a truthful index of a child's vocabulary. Likewise, if there is something about a test that causes scores to fluctuate wildly (e.g., questions which have several correct answers), a score from any one testing could not be considered a child's true score. If an IQ test is given in September, in all likelihood a different IQ score will be obtained if the same test is administered in October.

There is no way of knowing a child's true score on a test. Even conceptualizing the meaning of a true score can be difficult. We could administer a large number of tests, each with a different sample of questions, and use the average score to estimate how much an individual actually knew. Of course, the only way we would really know how much an individual knew would be to administer all possible questions. If this were attempted, the only question would be who would drop from exhaustion first: the test maker or the test taker. Another method for estimating a true score would be to readminister a test on several occasions. After twenty-five testings we might use a person's average score as an estimate of his/her true score. As with using tests having samples of different questions, this would cause fatigue in addition to a person's score on a test administered on successive occasions being affected by practice.

True scores cannot be determined, but by knowing how consistent or reliable a test is, general guidelines can be established to evaluate the accuracy of individual test scores. The process of determining how consistent or reliable a test is entails the calculation of a reliability coefficient.

Table XXII shows how a test-retest reliability coefficient is calculated. Ten children were given an IQ test in September and then retested in November. Using the method described in Chapter VII, the correlation between September and November

---

child received a score of 80, this child's estimated true score would be found by (1) subtracting the test mean from the score ($80 - 100 = -20$), (2) multiplying this deviation score by the reliability coefficient ($-20 \times .90 = -18$), and (3) adding this product to the mean of the test ($-18 + 100 = 82$). In this example the estimated true score is 82—though this is more a "best-guess-with-available-information" approach to truth rather than a method having a profound epistemological basis.

test scores was calculated. The correlation between test and retest scores was found to be 0.821. With a sample size of ten, a correlation must be greater than 0.765 to be significant at the .01 level. Although the test-retest correlation is statistically significant, there are still discrepancies between first and second test scores. As an example, Homer's IQ score increased by 20 points. No test score is immutable, especially IQ scores, and the less-than-perfect correlation simply signifies that scores can and did fluctuate.

TABLE XXII

EXAMPLE OF TEST-RETEST RELIABILITY

Child	September	November
Fred	125	120
Nancy	75	80
Gunther	95	85
Louie	120	115
Homer	80	100
Mary	110	105
Lefty	90	90
Herman	100	105
Jane	105	110
Tulip	100	90
Mean =	100	100
SD =	15.17	12.65
	$\Sigma XY = 101{,}575$	

$$r = \frac{\dfrac{101{,}575}{10} - (100)\,(100)}{(15.17)\,(12.65)}$$

$$r = 0.821$$

The terminology in measurement and statistics is often confusing, as demonstrated by referring to a correlation coefficient as a reliability coefficient. When scores from the same test are correlated, the coefficient is referred to as a reliability coefficient. This does not affect the manner or method by which the correlation was calculated. As suggested before, the correlation coefficient is a very versatile index.

A second method for calculating reliability is presented in Table XXIII. This example illustrates the calculation of reliability by the split-half method. As shown, a 6 item test was given to 5 children. A "0" indicates that an item was failed and a "1" signifies that an item was passed. For each child the sum of the odd items (items 1, 3, and 5) and the sum of the even items (2, 4, and 6) were determined. As an example (see Table XXIII), Louie answered 1 odd item correctly and 3 even items correctly. After the odd and even item sums had been found, the correlation between odd and even scores was determined. The correlation was found to be 0.737.

TABLE XXIII

EXAMPLE OF SPLIT-HALF RELIABILITY

Child	1	2	3	4	5	6	Odd Items	Even Items	Total
Jane	0	0	0	0	0	0	0	0	0
Homer	1	1	1	1	1	1	3	3	6
Fred	1	1	1	1	0	0	2	2	4
Louie	1	1	0	1	0	1	1	3	4
Mary	1	1	0	0	0	0	1	1	2

$$\text{Mean} = 1.40 \quad 1.80$$
$$SD = 1.02 \quad 1.17$$
$$\Sigma XY = 17$$

$$r = \frac{\dfrac{17}{5} - (1.40)(1.80)}{(1.02)(1.17)}$$
$$r = 0.737$$

Because the 6 item test was "split" in half between odd and even items (a usual but arbitrary decision), the correlation between odd and even items is only the reliability for half the test. The reliability for the whole test can be estimated by using what is called the Spearman-Brown formula:

$$\text{RELIABILITY} = \frac{2r_{o-e}}{1 + r_{o-e}}$$

where r_{o-e} is the correlation between odd and even items.

With an odd-even correlation of 0.737, the final estimate of this test's reliability is

$$\frac{2 \ (0.737)}{1 \ + \ (0.737)}$$

or 0.849.

There is no universal method for determining a test's reliability. Test-retest and internal consistency reliability coefficients might be reported, or one and not the other. For the most part internal-reliability coefficients will generally be higher than test-retest coefficients. Over a week, a month, or a year children will acquire new knowledge and new information, and they will approach a test for a second time from a different vantage point. If items on a test are drawn from the same area, internal consistency will be high. If the composition of a test is heterogeneous (e.g., items that measured personality traits, reading skill, and mechanical aptitude), internal consistency will be low. In this case test-retest will be more appropriate for estimating reliability than internal consistency. Also, internal consistency is inappropriate for speed tests which have a specific time limit, since restrictive time limits tend to inflate internal consistency estimates of reliability. Whichever method is used to estimate reliability, test scores will vary, a child's score can change, and no matter how revered the concept (e.g., IQ), nothing is constant.

STANDARD ERROR OF MEASUREMENT

If the reliability of a test were perfect, the score an individual received would be his/her true score. Remember, however, that truth is a many faceted concept, and it should not be interpreted to mean that a test is either useful or valid. In the same way that a reliability coefficient provides an overall estimate of a test's reliability, the standard error of measurement (SE_m) can be used to evaluate the "truthfulness" of a single test score. The standard error of measurement is equal to the standard deviation of a test times the square root of 1 minus the test's reliability. The formula for the standard error of measurement is

$$SE_m = SD \ \sqrt{1 - r_{tt}}$$

where SD is the standard deviation and r_{tt} signifies test reliability.

The standard error of measurement is often used to establish a band of confidence pertaining to an individual's true score.

If the reliability of a test was .90, and the standard deviation was 15, the standard error of measurement would be 4.74. The standard error of measurement is a standard deviation—but for interpreting an individual's score and not a group of individuals. As discussed before, one method for determining reliability would be to administer a large number of tests to an individual. Each testing might yield a different score, but the average score could be used as an estimate of reliability. If 100 tests were administered to an individual, the standard deviation of his scores would be the standard error of measurement. Just as in the normal distribution where 68 percent of the cases fall between one standard deviation above the mean and one standard deviation below the mean (see Table IX), 68 percent of an individual's scores will be between one standard error of measurement above and one standard error of measurement below the mean of a hypothetical group of scores.

If a child received an IQ score of 80 on a test with a standard deviation of 15, a reliability of .90, and a standard error of measurement of 5 (4.74 rounded), a statement could be made that 68 percent of the time this child's true score would be between 75 and 85.* If a test user wanted to be very certain of not overlooking a child's true score, a confidence band could be extended to two standard errors of measurement. Thus, in the above example, a two standard error of measurement band of confidence would indicate that 95 percent of the time a child's true score would fall between 70 and 90.

Reporting a child's true score on a test as being between certain limits is an excellent idea in that the possibility of test error is acknowledged. The problem arises when an assessment of a child's true score is used to imply a useful or valid score. A child's true score might be between 70 and 90. This, however,

---

* The band of confidence is actually around true scores. As an example, a standard error of measurement of 5 would indicate that a person's observed score would be between 5 points below and 5 points above his true score 68 percent of the time; or, a person's observed score would be between 10 points below and 10 points above his true score 95 percent of the time. The method for interpreting a standard error of measurement as described here deviates slightly from the traditional interpretation, but this method is commonly used and it will facilitate the interpretation of a persons test score or scores.

does not mean that we know more about the child, or that the test was not atrocious, or that the score can or will be used in some meaningful or beneficial way.

The shift from a statement about probable test error to meaningful or useful results often occurs when difference scores are found. If the means and standard deviations of two tests are similar, a test user might have reason to compare a child's test scores (e.g., comparing an arithmetic score to a reading score). One method for determining whether a difference between two test scores is significant is to use the standard error of measurement of difference scores (SE_{md}). This is found by first finding the standard error of measurement for each test being compared and then using the following formula:

$$SE_{md} = \sqrt{SE^2_{m_a} + SE^2_{m_b}}$$

where SE_m represents the standard error of measurement of the two tests (test A and B) being compared.

If the standard error of measurement for test A is 5 and the standard error of measurement for test B is 5, the standard error of measurement for the difference would be

$$\sqrt{5^2 + 5^2} = 7.07$$

If two tests had perfect reliability, the standard error of measurement of each test would be 0, and the standard error of measurement of difference scores would also be 0. On two such tests, if a child received a score of 10 on test A and a score of 9 on test B, the difference between these two scores (one point) would be a true difference; that is, a difference that was not the result of errors of measurement. The greater the difference between two test scores, in relation to the standard error of measurement of difference scores, the greater the possibility that the score difference was not the result of test error.

In the previous example, where the SE_{md} was about 7, most score differences (68%) would be equal to or less than seven points. Using 2 SM_{md}, 95 percent of score differences would be less than 14 points. A test user might use this information to state that a score difference less than 7 points was not significant; a score difference equal to or greater than 7 points but less than 14 points might not have been the result of chance; and a difference equal to or greater than 14 points was significant at the .05 level. If an individual received a score of 40 on test *A* and a score of 25 on test *B*, the score difference would be 15 points. Since 95 percent of score differences, in relation to a true score difference, will probably be less than 14 points, a score difference as great as 15 points is unusual and, as a result, is interpreted as being statistically significant.

When given a battery of tests or subtests, a child's scores will naturally vary. One test might be bead stringing and another head standing, and a score difference might be "statistically significant," but what would such a difference really mean? A score difference might be statistically interpreted as a significant difference (a difference that was not the result of test error), but that does not prove that the difference is abnormal or meaningful from a remedial standpoint. What is important is that tests be used to benefit and not to provide an opportunity for test users to play statistics. Difference scores have the potential of being useful, but they are not the most important or the most meaningful factors. Whenever a group statistic (e.g., reliability coefficient, SE_m, or SE_{md}) is used to interpret an individual score, and test scores are taken as infallible truth, the possibility of confusing a normal difference or normal performance with deviance or abnormal behavior is always present. A child is more than a set of test scores—a reality that will not be contravened by coefficients, significance, or test score differences.

INTERPRETATION OF RELIABILITY

Information relating to reliability is useful for understanding the internal consistency and stability of a test. In addition, reliability can be used to more realistically interpret individual scores (e.g., using SE_m). Possibly because of the fundamental importance of reliability, the mere act of reporting reliability coefficients is often taken as sufficient evidence that a test is reliable and valid.

In describing the Developmental Test of Visual Perception

(Maslow, Frostig, Lefever, and Whittlesey, 1964), test-retest reliabilities for the eye-motor coordination subtest were reported as ranging between .33 and .40 and split-half reliabilities as ranging between .59 and .60. The explanation for these low reliabilities was that "this subtest is affected much more than the other subtests by the physical condition and emotional state of the child existing at the moment of testing, as well as by environmental influences" (p. 489). The practice of simply reporting reliability coefficients and not interpreting them is common. If the reliability of a test is low, the test author should explicitly state that reliability is low and not substitute a bulk of statistics for a clear and straightforward interpretation.

In addition to ignoring or not interpreting a test's reliability, many professionals will confuse test reliability with test validity. A research project reported by Ratsunik and Koenigsknecht (1975) cited internal reliabiilty coefficients of .67 and .55 for an expressive-delayed language sample and a mentally retarded sample for the receptive section of the Northwestern Syntax Screening Test (Lee, 1971). Reliability coefficients of .78 and .81 were also cited for these same samples for the expressive subtest. These authors then stated that the receptive subtest "was a stable measure of syntactic and morphological decoding" and that the expressive subtest "was a stable measure of syntactic and morphological encoding" (p. 63). What actually was reported were relatively low reliability coefficients, which did not demonstrate that either the receptive or expressive subtest measured syntactic or morphological decoding or encoding. Whether a test is internally consistent is a question of reliability; what a test measures, or whether it measures what it claims to measure is a matter of validity.

Reliability coefficients can be used to estimate the stability of scores over a period of time, and as an indicator of possible sources of error (e.g., too few test items, ambiguous items or instructions, or dissimilar items for a supposedly homogeneous test). Once reliability has been determined, a frequently asked question is how high test reliability should be. An Educational Testing Service booklet ("Short-cut statistics," 1964) stated that "test publishers have traditionally not been satisfied with reliabilities less than .90 . . ." (p. 31). Mehrens and Lehmann (1973) stated that "although there is no universal agreement, it is generally accepted that standardized tests used to assist in making decisions about individuals should have reliability coefficients of at least .85" (p. 122). Nunnally (1967) stated that "in those applied settings where important decisions are made with respect to specific test scores, a reliability of .90 is the minimum that should be tolerated, and a reliability of .95 should be considered the desirable standard" (p. 226). Colarusso and Hammill (1972) introduced a test called the Motor-Free Visual Perception Test and reported reliability coefficients (test-retest and internal consistency) ranging between .71 and .84. They then stated that "coefficients of 0.80 or above are traditionally accepted as evidence of adequate test reliability" (p. 14). What all this suggests is that test reliability should be greater than 0.90—but lower estimates might be accepted depending upon whether you are a test user or test maker.

For a test user to understand a test, information pertaining to reliability is essential. However, when reliability is used as a cosmetic, when coefficients are reported for the sake of reporting and no real attempt is made to understand errors of measurement, few will profit, least of all the children for whom a test was intended.

Chapter Thirteen

THE IMAGE OF TESTING

PROFIT FACTORS

Educational testing has an image of professionalism, objectivity, statistical accuracy, and necessity. Proponents of testing will grudgingly concede that the reporting of test results can be cruel, but they will also note that persons are constantly being tested—including career, social, and academic advancement—and that testing is a way of life, a natural method for selecting, categorizing, and rewarding students. What is more, they will add, testing can be used to understand a child and to mold an appropriate educational program.

The image of educational testing portrays the child as the benefactor of assessment and evaluation. This image acts as buffer between the practice of testing and potential critics of testing. Criticizing a picayune aspect of testing might be tolerated or even encouraged (e.g., circular arguments concerning correlations), but criticizing the overall intent of educational testing is to criticize what is good for children! Righteous proponents of testing would not condone that.

There is a difference between the reality of testing and the image of testing. In the reality of testing, children are often victims rather than beneficiaries. Furthermore, by no stretch of the imagination are persons tested either the sole or primary beneficiaries of testing. Every individual involved with testing profits. This includes test makers, test publishers, and test users. Test takers may profit, but not always in a way that is positive or beneficial.

The beginning point of a standardized test is often with a university professor. This person, having expertise in measurement and testing or a content area (e.g., reading, mathematics), constructs a test for altruistic purposes, to make a contribution to the field of education, to obtain notoriety, or to make money. These do not exhaust the possibilities of why a test is conceived and developed, and a realistic assessment of the incipient motivation behind a test would probably reveal a combination of factors: a need for scholarly production ("publish or perish"), a desire to create, and a pecuniary awareness of the limitations of a university professor's salary. The point to be made is that the profits reaped by test developers are not limited to the satisfaction of knowing that a child has somehow benefited.

Where the test developer provides an idea and professorial dignity, the test publisher provides technical know-how, production, and marketing savvy. The image of educational testing as being professional is generated by titular association (Would a Ph.D. construct a test that was not professional?); the reality of educational testing is the fact that it is a business.

Most educational tests are not free. A test buyer might be able to obtain a DO NOT DISTURB—TESTING sign at no cost, but most tests, if not all tests, must be purchased. The cost of a single test, complete with "sturdy" carrying case, might range between twenty and seventy dollars. The price of a group test or testing program will depend upon the number of test forms ordered (the cost per form is usually inexpensive and might range between $0.20 and $0.40), manuals and supplementary materials requested (e.g., answer sheets, scoring keys), and whether tests are scored by the user or publisher. When the extent of testing in the United States is visualized, from preschool assessment to graduate school entrance examinations, and when the diversity of testing is considered, the amount of money involved in educational testing is astronomical.

Whenever an investment is made and a return expected, the possibility exists that concern for that investment (e.g., producing and marketing a test) will exceed professional and moral responsibilities. Tests are developed, manufactured, and marketed because there is a demand and because a profit can be made. In most circumstances a test publisher would not knowingly publish a test that was deceptive, destructive, or had the potential for doing untold harm. However, the publisher of a test makes no pretense about being an expert or authority, and so reliance is placed on the goodwill and professional responsibility of the test developer (i.e., the university professor). The test maker, on the other hand, is not concerned about the mercenary world of publishing, and so advertising hyperboles, test misuses, and idiotic test decisions made on the basis of test results are ignored.

Next, varied types of test users profit from educational tests. A user might profit by having a test that no one else can give, thus enabling an individual to operate as a much-needed specialist. A second type of test user might not administer tests directly but instead use test information to make decisions (e.g., assign children to reading groups, categorize children as being retarded). A third type of test user might not be interested in practical applications of test information but is more concerned about the statistical (e.g., reliability) characteristics of a test. This type of user, usually a university professor, contributes to the image of educational testing as being professional by suggesting that tests are rigorously monitored and evaluated. The primary profit gained by a person who evaluates a test and publishes that evaluation in a Journal is in having another two or three lines to add to his or her vita. Evaluations of tests appearing in Journals cannot be too honest, for that would be construed as being too unprofessional, and they must be suitably laced with statistics, for to do otherwise would also demonstrate a high degree of unprofessionalism. The results of this are whitewashing expositions of tests, which are brimming with statistics and which can only be understood by other professionals.

Finally, a child might benefit from an educational test. When a test is studied, evaluated, and honestly interpreted, and if children are thought of as being more than test scores, a test might be very helpful in understanding why and how a child behaves. The difficulty with educational tests does not concern the potential value of tests—used judiciously and thoughtfully many tests can be of considerable value—but concerns mistaking the image of testing for the reality of testing and assuming that the only purpose of an educational test is to better fulfill and maximize the individual needs of children.

THE MYSTIQUE OF TESTING

"The image is a pseudo-event . . . it is synthetic, believable, passive, vivid, simplified and ambiguous." Boorstin's (1961, p. 185) description of an image is an apt characterization of how educational tests are perceived. But there is something about testing, an attribute inherent in standardized tests, that inexorably binds test maker, publisher, user, and taker. Tests are drenched in secrecy. Test content is secret, test performance is secret, only a few are privy to test information, and even fewer are aware of how test information is actually being used.

The mystery associated with educational testing is a product of practical, ethical, and professional considerations. A child soon learns that the penalty for peering at another's multiple-choice markings can be great. During many mass testing situations it is as if invisible hands held heads bent by the nape of the neck. If little trust is extended during testing, absolutely none is offered once testing is completed. Feedback and reporting test performance might have a sound educational basis, but revealing the content of a test could result in a number of unsavory practices (e.g., kindergarten children stealthily recording questions and correct answers with the intent of profit at a later date).

If becoming a doctor, lawyer, or Ph.D. is contingent on receiving an acceptable grade on a multiple-choice test, there is good reason to believe that desperate and cautious students would go to great pains to obtain a copy of test questions. The need to create a test for a great many individuals, and yet make a profit, has resulted in the unique American testing experience: an anxiety-riddled, tension-loaded two to three hours of selecting one of four possible choices, during which time the purpose and quality of an individual's life can be determined.

As if withholding specific test performance were not enough, many test users also guard against revealing all test information, including overall test scores. The rationale for this is that a child would not understand test information and that a parent might misinterpret test information. This seemingly benevolent philosophy has resulted in educational tests being used to make important decisions without a parent, guardian, or advocate being able to challenge inaccurate or misleading information. Fortunately, the Family Educational Rights and Privacy Act of 1974 has attempted to counter some of the more serious abuses by stipulating that a parent or guardian has a right to inspect a child's school records and to be able to challenge the legitimacy of dubious data. Failure of an institution to comply with these regulations can result in denial of federal financial assistance. To what extent this law will affect the use and interpretation of test data remains to be seen. At the very least, the possibility of accountability may guard against the inhouse use of fictitious labels (e.g., IQ) and illusory information.

Insofar as test content, test performance, and test scores are recondite, it is not surprising that only a few professionals, learned in the ancient ways of testing, are allowed to gather and interpret test data. Reading teachers give reading tests; speech teachers give speech and language tests; psychologists give psychological tests; special education teachers have a reputation for giving wide-range and perceptual-motor tests; and classroom teachers are left with the ritual of group testing by decree of principal or assistant principal.

Although the use of specialized personnel to administer and interpret tests further contributes to the mystique of educational testing ("Have him tested by——to determine whether he is ——."), no one would want an unqualified person to administer whatever struck his or her fancy. This, of course, does happen (e.g., IQ tests being given by nonpsychologists, achievement tests being given by persons who know nothing about achievement, and language tests being given by everyone).

There is no denying that trained specialists can best interpret specific aspects of a child's behavior. However, the notion that a child's behavior can be broken down into three, four, or more parts is completely unrealistic. A child is complex, and areas of language, achievement, psychological makeup, and personality are inextricably related. The problem is further compounded when each specialist administers a battery of standardized tests as if each child were a linear combination of test scores. There are schools where professionals do gather as a team and share information to further meet the educational needs of a child. In other settings professional elitism and snobbery create the impression that a child can be shuffled about until an answer is found.

The rise of the test expert, arcane skills and all, can be attributed to a concern for possible abuse by unskilled and irresponsible persons. An unwanted by-product of this concern is a system of testing that diffuses and shifts responsibility. Each specialist has a unique skill or area to assess; if a child is not understood or not behaving as expected, absolution for not trying to understand a child can be had by referring said child to a specialist or an expert. After all, the reasoning goes, the specialist can find out what is wrong.

There are experts, test specialists, who will do their utmost to understand a child, who will advocate a child's interests beyond the normal call of duty and beyond all professional expectations. And then, there are those who do not. A teacher once found a second grade boy to be somewhat overactive. The boy was reading about a year below grade level, so she requested that a psychologist be called in to determine whether the child had a learning problem. The psychologist administered a well-known individual test of intelligence (not the entire test) and proceeded to inform the parents of the bad news: their child had an IQ of 74, and he was recommending placement in a class with children said to be mentally retarded. The psychologist did not consult with the classroom teacher, resource room teacher, or the reading teacher because he was leary of the team approach. He was, as demonstrated by his state certification, the expert. After knowing a child for forty-five minutes and consulting with no one, he categorized a child as being mentally retarded. School personnel were shocked; the teacher was shocked; the parents were shocked. The psychologist responded to this unanimous amazement by declaring that the school and parents did not want to face reality. More specifically, he accused school personnel of not wanting to "give up" one of their children. This scenario does not typify school psychologists, there are school psychologists who would give an arm and a leg for the rights and needs of a child, but only serves to caution that no area is so venerable, no testing so mysterious and above reproach that the fate of a child can go unchallenged. As of this writing, the child described is still in a regular class and continues to learn to read, write, spell, and play with his friends.

BURDEN OF PROOF

For the most part, educational tests have been viewed as being a positive and necessary force in American education; the view has been that a critic of a test or test score needed to defend dissatisfaction or general misgivings. All tests and test scores must be presumed to be useless and misleading. The test user or the advocate for the test taker need not show that a test is worthless; it is the responsibility of the test maker to demonstrate, to prove that a test or test score is useful or somehow beneficial. Too often, tests are published with little or no information showing their value or even basic information concerning validity (e.g., correlations). The premise is that a score need not be proven useful, but that it must be shown to be in error before it is discounted. This is wrong. If a child is labeled as being retarded, he must be proven to be retarded. If a test claims to measure intelligence, it must be proven to measure intelligence. If a test is designed to measure achievement, it must be shown to measure achievement. The burden of proof is on the test maker or test promoter to demonstrate the efficacy of a test or score and not on the test taker or test user.

With an attitude that educational tests are fallible, scores can be misinterpreted, and horrendous decisions can be made on the basis of test information, a beginning is at hand to disentangle the reality of testing from the image of testing. The next step is to seek information pertaining to the meaning of a score or test. Why was the test selected? Is test content meaningful? What are the test's psychometric characteristics (e.g., reliability and validity)? What are the test's assets and limitations? How is test information being used? How does a child benefit from having been tested?

There are a variety of sources for obtaining information relating to tests and test scores. A good starting point is the person who selected the test, followed by the test user, and then the recipient of test information (e.g., parents, teachers, and administrators). The test itself and the test manual are invaluable for determining the rationale and potential usefulness of a test. A thorough reading of a test or test manual might be taken for granted, but frequently test users fail to scrutinize either test content or technical information contained in test manuals. A feeling for a test can often be had by reading test reviews, which are occasionally published in professional Journals as well as in Buros' *Mental Measurements Yearbook*. Technical articles can be informative, but too often they are more concerned about statistical protocol than evaluating the underlying worth of a test. For a descriptive account of tests, textbooks can be useful, although these often pander to advertised test blessings rather than attempting to present an objective assessment of a test.

Skepticism, suspicion, objectivity, honesty, effort, perseverance, information, and more information—these are the rudiments for seeing through the image of educational testing. At first sight the reality of testing might be traumatic, but as an awareness for what educational testing is takes hold, the greatest beneficiaries will be the children evaluated.

Chapter Fourteen

THE POTENTIAL OF TESTING

IN DEFENSE OF TESTING

S CORES, TESTS, AND statistics have been discussed, but what can finally be said about testing? What of Ebel's (1975) statement that "tests have the potential to do much more good than harm in our society. Looked at impartially, that is what the record will show that they have done" (p. 95). Indeed, what does the asset side of the ledger show?

Tests are objective. There is no question that an optical scanner will score tests (read and count correct multiple-choice markings) with greater accuracy than an individual could read and score essay questions.

Tests are capable of discriminating among individuals. More than a few psychometricians believe that a test that does not discriminate is not a good test. Submerged in this idea is the belief that discriminating among individuals will be good for child, school, and society.

Standardized tests are efficient. This might be the greatest asset that testing has to offer. For an extremely small fee, decisions can be made regarding the labeling, grouping, or rewarding of a child.

Tests can be used to evaluate and track a child's performance. Even a mediocre test will give a rough idea as to the educational progress of a child. If the testing program is the least bit coherent, a child's academic performance can be monitored over a period of years.

Tests can be used to diagnose individual learning difficulties. Some tests can assist in determining a child's academic, personal, and psychological needs.

Tests can be used to hold teachers accountable for what they are teaching. Although tests are used in a very limited way to evaluate teacher effectiveness, extensive use of educational tests for this purpose would surely result in teachers teaching tests. In addition, teacher unions would never stand for it.

There are untold ancillary benefits associated with educational testing. Absolutely! Testing is a multimillion dollar industry in which many individuals profit. Testing provides a means for removing a child from the regular classroom. Testing provides a wealth of information for government reports, papers, and documents. Testing offers a cost-effective method for grouping (e.g., reading groups), categorizing (e.g., retarded and nonretarded), and rewarding (e.g., scholarships) individuals. Testing can be used to justify educational decisions. Testing can be used to establish the importance of an educational program by serving as a door to graduation, certification, and accreditation.

Words like *good* and *harm* are relative terms, but educational tests do have their uses.

THE OTHER SIDE OF TESTING

There is no black and white to educational testing, and definitely no grand ledger or tally sheet to compare the benefits and limitations of tests, test scores, and testing practices. The often-touted objectivity of tests is, paradoxically, far from being clear-cut. A test can have dubious validity and still be objective— objective in the sense that an individual's test score will not vary drastically as a result of test examiner or test scorer. The objective nature of standardized tests is not without merit, but too often this concept of objectivity is used as breastwork to stave off crticisms, to escape responsibility, and to reinforce environmental inequities. A typical rejoinder is "standardized tests are objective and therefore the best method for evaluation and assessment." This argument deceptively ignores the more basic question that what is being assessed might be unnecessary or that the information being obtained might be useless.

One of the more despicable practices in testing is to use objectivity as a vehicle to escape responsibility. "The test shows that he is retarded"; "The test proves that he is not achieving"; "The test demonstrates that he has a serious problem." An individual need not make a decision when responsibility can be shifted to a test, an inanimate object. If an error is made, the test was responsible and not the test maker, test publisher, or test user. Decision making is part of reality, but when a decision is made concerning a human being, another individual, or an identifiable group of individuals, must assume full and complete responsibility.

Protests that educational tests are culturally biased are often greeted with the assertion that tests simply measure skills, knowledge, and competencies necessary to exist in society. This type of reasoning acts to perpetuate racial stereotypes and environmental differences. As an example, an individual has a low vocabulary as a result of environmental influences; this person is categorized as having a low IQ; the educational response to this low IQ is lowered expectations, watered-down curricula, and fewer opportunities. Testing insures that an individual is further handicapped from reaching his or her potential.

Akin to the problem of educational tests being used to maintain racial and class distinctions, there are always specific instances of tests being used to admit (e.g., to schools, trade unions), qualify, or certify an individual on the basis of something other than competence or potential competence. As an example, a black is denied being a journeyman bricklayer on the basis of a paper-pencil test rather than being judged on bricklaying and bricklaying-related skills.

Standing alongside objectivity as the *raison d'etre* of educational testing is the ability of tests to discriminate among individuals. There are benefits to be gained from discriminating among individuals (e.g., as an aid to identifying a child's strengths and weaknesses). The major problem is the use of tests to discriminate and then categorize children. Once a child has been categorized, the child will likely remain in that category for the duration of his/her formal education. The test on which the initial decision to categorize was made might have been in error or not sensitive to natural developmental differences, but placing a child in a category (e.g., retarded category, low reading group, slow track) will place restrictions on the quality and complexity of instruction, as well as teacher expectations, so as to make advancement to a higher category more difficult with increasing time. Saying that a child can always advance to a higher group is a debasement of the truth. Once a child has been categorized, the realities of that category and what is expected of a person in that category will operate to promote permanent group membership.

As has already been implied, there are no clear-cut answers, no good or bad, no absolutes when discussing the assets and limitations of educational tests. Tests are efficient, but they can also be destructive. Tests can be used to track a child's educational performance, but the information stored might be misleading. Tests can be used to diagnose learning problems, but often mythical problems are detected and nonsensical remedial programs proposed.

There is a bottling plant in Chicago where soft drinks are produced and distributed. After the bottles are washed, filled, and cased, they are sent down a conveyor to an automatic loader. Should one of the wooden cases hit a snag or somehow impede the flow, rather than stopping the line, an operator rushes over and literally throws the case off the line so that bottles, cartons, and case splatter to the floor. This might seem to be a waste of bottles, but no doubt someone determined that this was more efficient and cost-effective than halting the line and correcting the problem. Educational testing is much the same. Someone determines an arbitrary cutoff, and those below that point are thrown out of the flow—an achievement score is too low, an IQ score is too low, a score on a medical college admission test is too low. Errors might be made, at times the cutoffs might be too high or too low, some will suffer and others will be denied opportunities, and the difference might be as trivial as a lucky or unlucky guess on a multiple-choice test, but someone decided that in the long run this was the most efficient and cost-effective method for maintaining a constant educational flow. Is this good? Is it bad? Whatever it is, it certainly suggests a peculiar concept of morality.

RESPONSIBILITY AND EDUCATIONAL TESTING

The full meaning and usefulness of educational testing will only be realized when professionals and nonprofessionals assume responsibilities too long neglected. At the development level, persons who construct tests have a responsibility to be objective and honest and to exhibit a high degree of scholarly integrity. The usefulness and limitations of a test should be evaluated prior to public dissemination, and specific instructions should be given as to how a test should be used and how it can be abused. The American Psychological Association's manual entitled *Standards for Educational and Psychological Tests and Manuals* (1966) offers the following advice to test makers:

> The test user needs information to help him select the test that is most adequate for a given purpose, and most of that information must come from the test producer. The practices of authors and publishers in furnishing information have varied. With some tests, the user is offered directions for administering and scoring the test, norms of uncertain origin, and virtually nothing more. In contrast, other tests have manuals that furnish extensive information on their development, their validity and reliability, the bases for their norms, the kinds of interpretation that are appropriate, and the uses for which the tests can best be employed. (p. 7)

A test maker's responsibilities consist of more than promoting pet theories, item writing, and royalties. A test maker is responsible for bad decisions made on the basis of a bad test, for misinterpretations resulting from shallow conceptualization, and for abuses caused by a lack of information. When an individual constructs a test, responsibility does not end with its publication.

Heretofore, test publishers have assumed a businesslike posture regarding educational tests and have relinquished all responsibility for the value of a test to the test maker. The primary person responsible for a test and the results that a test brings is the test maker, but test publishers have a responsibility to be responsive to test criticisms and to demand that a test or test information be modified so as not to distort or mislead. There are occasions when professionals are unanimous in the opinion that a test has no redeeming merit, yet the test publisher remains oblivious to cries for a test's reconstruction, modification, or withdrawal from public consumption. A test maker might be unable to acknowledge the possibility that a test developed was worthless or even harmful, but a test publisher cannot remain aloof from a test that can yield misinformation and anguish.

The responsibilities of test makers and publishers should

not overshadow the importance or magnitude of obligations incurred by test users. For professionals who use tests in order to evaluate their usefulness or psychometric characteristics, a responsibility for honesty is assumed. Test reviews and technical articles are usually meek descriptions and/or glorified actuarial accounts. If there is a pernicious element in educational testing, it exists because professionals have allowed it to exist. A professional, a Ph.D., has the responsibility of being honest, of being objective, of stating that "This test is not worth the paper it's printed on!" if a test deserves as much. One reviewer or researcher might disagree with another, but both should be honest, state what they believe, and reveal the facts for what they are. Professionals cannot afford to be restricted by "professional restraint" and concern for a test maker's feelings. If a test was designed for use with a child, then the child and not the test maker should be the focal point of concern.

A test maker should realize that his or her reputation is being placed on the line when a test is offered for public use. Tampering with the lives of children is serious business. After all, the responsibility involved in the creation of a test that can be used to classify children as being retarded is awesome. If an error in classification is made because of a test, does one say, "Oops! Sorry about that life. No test is perfect"? Persons who evaluate tests should let it be known that deception will not be tolerated and that accountability will be exacted.

For clinicians, specialists, and teachers, a responsibility exists to understand what is being tested and to use information with a relentless concern for the child. Test users cannot afford the luxury of assuming that a test is good or that a test is valid. A test must be understood, its construction must be understood, its uses and possible abuses must be undertood, and how it can best be used to help a child must be understood. Accepting test claims at face value is irresponsible; using tests mechanistically is inhuman; and interpreting test information without a complete concern for the child is reckless.

Finally, for those who receive test information for decision-making purposes (e.g., teachers, administrators), a responsibility exists to regard a child as being more than a score and to advocate programs that will accommodate a child's skill and potential and not performance on a test.

Educational tests are not sacred. All who come in contact with tests and test scores have a responsibility to evaluate their substance and meaning and not to be frightened or bamboozled by a plethora of statistics or erudite psychometrics. Only when there is honesty and objectivity, only when information is sought and questions freely asked will children prevail over educational testing.

*   *   *   *   *

"Stop!" She orders.
Pencil down, hands folded, wait and watch the teacher.
"Pass your tests forward."
Pass tests, bell, time to go.
"Bye, Mrs. Posner."
"Goodbye, Johnny. See you tomorrow."
Out door, down hall, past office, past gym and cafeteria. A stream of kids holding the glass door open. The sun is bright; squint; a soft throb just above the left eye.
"Hi."
"Hi."
"How'd you do?"
Look at the sidewalk, and then see the yellow school bus, and then I'm home.

BIBLIOGRAPHY

Adkins, Dorothy C.: *Test Construction* (2nd ed.). Columbus, Ohio: Charles E. Merrill, 1974.

Anastasi, Anne: Psychology, psychologists, and psychological testing. *Am Psychol*, 1967, *22*:297-306.

Beatty, Leslie S., Madden, Richard, and Gardner, Eric F.: *Stanford Diagnostic Arithmetic Test* (Level II). New York: Harcourt, Brace & World, 1966.

Blommers, Paul and Lindquist, E. F.: *Elementary Statistical Methods.* Boston: Houghton Mifflin Company, 1960.

Boorstin, Daniel J.: *The Image.* New York: Harper & Row, 1961.

Buros, Oscar K. (Ed.): *The Seventh Mental Measurements Yearbook.* Highland Park, New Jersey: Gryphon Press, 1972.

Carroll, John B.: Review of the Illinois Test of Psycholinguistic Abilities. In Oscar K. Buros (Ed.): *Seventh Mental Measurements Yearbook.* Highland Park, New Jersey: Gryphon Press, 1972.

Carroll, Lewis: *Alice's Adventures in Wonderland.* Macmillan, 1868. In *The Annotated Alice,* with an introduction and notes by Martin Gardner. New York: World Publishing Company, 1960, p. 95.

Chase, Clinton I.: Review of the Illinois Test of Psycholinguistic Abilities. In Oscar K. Buros (Ed.): *Seventh Mental Measurements Yearbook.* Highland Park, New Jersey: Gryphon Press, 1972.

Colarusso, Ronald P. and Hammill, Donald D.: *Motor-Free Visual Perception Test.* San Rafael, California: Academic Therapy Publications, 1972.

Connolly, Austin J., Nachtman, William, and Pritchett, E. Milo: *KeyMath Diagnostic Arithmetic Test.* Circle Pines, Minnesota: American Guidance Service, 1971.

Cronbach, Lee. J.: *Essentials of Psychological Testing* (3rd ed.). New York: Harper & Row, 1970.

Delacato, Carl H.: *Neurological Organization and Reading.* Springfield, Illinois: Charles C Thomas, 1966.

Doll, Edgar A.: *Vineland Social Maturity Scale.* Circle Pines, Minnesota: American Guidance Service, 1965.

Dunn, Lloyd M.: *Peabody Picture Vocabulary Test.* Circle Pines, Minnesota: American Guidance Service, 1965.

Dunn, Lloyd M. and Markwardt, Fredrick C.: *Peabody Individual Achievement Test.* Circle Pines, Minnesota: American Guidance Service, 1970.

Durost, Walter N. (Ed.): *Metropolitan Achievement Tests* (Primary I Battery). New York: Harcourt, Brace & World, 1959.

Ebel, Robert L.: The social consequences of educational testing. In Victor H. Noll, Dale P. Scannell, and Rachel P. Noll (Eds.): *Introductory Readings in Educational Measurement.* Boston: Houghton Mifflin Company, 1972. (Reprinted from *School and Society,* 1964, 331-334.)

Ebel, Robert L.: Comments on Green's attack on tests & testing. *Phi Delta Kappan,* 1975, 57, 93.

Family Educational Rights and Privacy Act, 1974, P.L. 93-380, section 438 (20 U.S.C. 1232-g).

Freeman, Frank S.: *Theory and Practice of Psychological Testing* (3rd ed.). New York: Holt, Rinehart and Winston, 1962.

Frostig, Marianne; Lefever, Welty, and Whittlesey, John R.: *Developmental Test of Visual Perception* (Rev ed.). Palo Alto, California: Consulting Psychologist Press, 1966.

Goslin, David A.: *Teachers and Testing.* New York: Russell Sage Foundation, 1967.

Green, Robert L.: Tips on educational testing: what teachers & parents should know. *Phi Delta Kappan,* 1975, 57:89-93.

Gronlund, Norman E.: *Readings in Measurement and Evaluation.* New York: The Macmillan Company, 1968.

Guilford, J. P.: Psychometric Methods (2nd ed.). New York: McGraw-Hill Book Company, 1954.

Guilford, J. P.: *Fundamental Statistics in Psychology and Education* (4th ed.). New York: McGraw-Hill Book Company, 1965.

Hildreth, Gertrude H., Griffiths, Nellie L., and McGauvran, Mary E.: *Metropolitan Readiness Tests.* New York: Harcourt, Brace & World, 1969.

Hoffman, Banesh: *The Tyranny of Testing.* New York: Crowell-Collier-Macmillan, 1962.

Jensen, Arthur R.: How much can we boost IQ and scholastic achievement? *Harvard Educational Review,* 1969, 39:1-123.

Johnson, G. O.: Special education for the mentally retarded—a paradox. *Except Child,* 1962, 29:62-69.

Kerlinger, Fred N.: *Foundations of Behavioral Research* (2nd ed.). New York: Holt, Rinehart and Winston, 1973.

Kirk, Samuel A., McCarthy, James J., and Kirk, Winifred D.: *Illinois Test of Psycholinguistic Abilities* (Rev. ed.). Urbana, Illinois: University of Illinois Press, 1968.

Lee, Laura: *Northwestern Syntax Screening Test.* Evanston, Illinois: Northwestern University Press, 1971.

Lorge, Irving, and Thorndike, Robert L.: *The Lorge-Thorndike Intelligence Tests.* Boston: Houghton Mifflin Company, 1957.

Lyman, Howard B.: *Test Scores and What They Mean* (2nd ed.). New Jersey: Prentice-Hall, 1971.

Maslow, Phyllis, Frostig, Marianne, Lefever, D. W., and Whittlesey, John R.: The Marianne Frostig Developmental Test of Visual Perception 1963 Standardization. *Percept Mot Skills*, 1964, *19*:463-499.

Mehrens, William A. and Lehmann, Irvin J.: *Measurement and Evaluation in Education and Psychology*. New York: Holt, Rinehart and Winston, 1973.

Noll, Victor H., Scannell, Dale P., and Noll, Rachel, P. (Eds.): *Introductory Readings in Educational Measurement*. Boston: Houghton Mifflin Company, 1972.

Nunnally, Jum C.: *Psychometric Theory*. New York: McGraw-Hill, 1967.

Otis, Arthur S.: *Statistical Method in Educational Measurement*. Chicago: World Book Company, 1925.

Paraskevopoulous, John N. and Kirk, Samuel A.: *The Development and Psychometric Characteristics of the Revised Illinois Test of Psycholinguistic Abilities*. Urbana, Illinois: University of Illinois Press, 1969.

Ratusnik, David L. and Koenigsknecht, Roy A.: Internal consistency of the Northwestern Syntax Screening Test. *J Speech Hear Disord*, 1975, *40*:59-68.

Roach, Eugene G., and Kephart, Newell C.: *The Purdue Perceptual-Motor Survey*. Columbus, Ohio: Charles E. Merrill, 1966.

Robinson, Halbert B., and Robinson, Nancy M.: *The Mentally Retarded Child*. New York: McGraw-Hill Book Company, 1965.

Rosenthal, Robert and Jacobson, Lenore: *Pygmalion in the Classroom*. New York: Holt, Rinehart and Winston, 1968.

Ross, Sterling, L., DeYoung, Henry G., and Cohen, Julius S.: Confrontation: special education placement and the law. *Except Child*, 1971, *38*:5-12.

Runyon, Richard P., and Haber, Audrey: *Fundamentals of Behavioral Statistics*. Reading, Massachusetts: Addison-Wesley Publishing Company, 1967.

Short-cut Statistics for Teacher-made Tests. Princeton, New Jersey: Educational Testing Service, 1960.

Smith, B. O.: *Logical Aspects of Educational Measurement*. New York: Columbia University Press, 1938.

Standards for Educational and Psychological Tests and Manuals: John W. French and William B. Michael, Cochairmen. Washington: American Psychological Association, 1966.

Stern, William: *General Psychology*, translated by Howard Davis Spoerl. New York: The Macmillan Company, 1938.

Terman, Lewis M. and Merrill, Maud A.: *Measuring Intelligence*. Boston: Houghton Mifflin Company, 1937.

Terman, Lewis M. and Merrill, Maud A.: *Stanford-Binet Intelligence Scale* (Rev. ed.). Boston: Houghton Mifflin Company, 1960.

Terman, Lewis M. and Merrill, Maud A.: *Stanford-Binet Intelligence Scale* (Rev. ed.). Boston: Houghton Mifflin Company, 1973.

Thorndike, Robert L.: Review of *Pygmalion in the Classroom* by Robert Rosenthal and Lenore Jacobson. *American Educational Research Journal,* 1968, 5:708-711.

Tiegs, Ernest W. and Clark, Willis W.: *California Achievement Tests* Monterey, California: CTB/McGraw-Hill, 1970.

Webster's New Collegiate Dictionary: Springfield, Massachusetts: G & C. Merriam Company, 1976.

Wechsler, David: *Wechsler Intelligence Scale for Children.* New York: The Psychological Corporation, 1949.

Wechsler, David: *Wechsler Intelligence Scale for Children—Revised.* New York: The Psychological Corporation, 1974.

INDEX

A

Academic achievement, 59
  grade equivalents and, 60-67
Adkins, Dorothy, 110, 124
Age equivalents, 60
American Psychological Association, 154
Anastasi, Anne, 3
Average, 28, 29
  departure from, 30, 31
  mean as, 30
  standard deviation and, 31-35

B

Bandwidth-fidelity dilemma, 96
Beatty, Leslie, 75
Boorstin, Daniel, 145
Buros, Oscar, 93, 149

C

California Achievement Test, 92
Carroll, John, 93
Carroll, Lewis, 99
Causation, 111-115
  circular reasoning and, 89, 90
  faulty reasoning and, 111, 112
Chase, Clinton, 95
Clark, Willis, 92
Cohen, Julius, 57
Colarusso, Ronald, 141
Connolly, Austin, 95
Correlation, 77-90
  calculation of, 82-85
  curvilinear, 80
  defined, 77
  graphic description of, 79, 81

linear, 80
negative, 80
positive, 77
prediction and, 85
significance of, 88
validity and, 89
Criterion-referenced tests, 74-76
Cronbach, Lee, 12, 60, 96

D

Delacato, Carl, 115
Developmental Test of Visual
    Perception, 114, 139
DeYoung, Henry, 57
Diana v. State Board of Education, 57
Distributions,
  frequency, examples of, 16, 18, 21,
    22, 25
  normal curve and, 55-57
  skewed, 24-26
  symmetrical, 20-21
Doll, Edgar, 97
Dunn, Lloyd, 55, 66, 73, 92
Durost, Walter, 60

E

Ebel, Robert, 12, 47, 150
Educable mentally retarded, 120
Educational Testing Service, 140

F

Family Educational Rights and
    Privacy Act, 146
Frequencies (*see* Distributions)
Frostig, Marianne, 114, 140

161